BEYOND THE DROP ZONE

Beyond the Drop Zone

I, Andrew Williams, hereby assert and give notice of my rights under Section 77 of the Copyright, Design, and Patents Act, 1988 to be identified as the author of this work.

All rights reserved. No part of this publication may be reproduced, stored in a retrieval system or transmitted at any time by any means electronic, mechanical, photocopying, recording, or otherwise, without prior permission of the publisher.

© 2024, Andrew Williams

All rights reserved.

ISBN: 9798335348317

DEDICATION

To those who paid the ultimate sacrifice in war, allowing us the precious gift of freedom, and to those enduring the psychological toll of conflict far from the battlefield—this book is dedicated to you, a testament to your sacrifice and a beacon of gratitude. Your bravery and resilience will forever inspire us. Finally, to my remarkable sister, who selflessly gave up her childhood to raise me as her own and has saved my life in more ways than one.

In Flanders Fields

By John McCrae

In Flanders fields the poppies blow
Between the crosses, row on row,
That mark our place; and in the sky
The larks, still bravely singing, fly
Scarce heard amid the guns below.

We are the Dead. Short days ago
We lived, felt dawn, saw sunset glow,
Loved and were loved, and now we lie,
In Flanders fields.

Take up our quarrel with the foe:
To you from failing hands we throw
The torch; be yours to hold it high.
If ye break faith with us who die
We shall not sleep, though poppies grow
In Flanders fields.

Beyond the Drop Zone

CONTENTS

	Introduction	1
	Prologue	3
1	Roots and Beginnings	5
2	The Path Chosen	19
3	Battalion Life	30
4	The Troubles	36
5	Operation Telic	43
6	The Graveyard of Empires	50
7	Platoon House	59
8	The Longest Day	67
9	Amidst the Whirlwind	77
10	The War Has Come Home	99
11	A New Mission	115
12	The Hornet's Nest	124
13	The Hidden Eye	133
14	Fighting the Abyss	140
15	Love's Unexpected Arrival	148
16	The Fire Service	152
17	Quest for Purpose	158

Beyond the Drop Zone

ACKNOWLEDGEMENTS

First and foremost, I wish to express my deepest gratitude to my wife, Louise. Your unwavering support and encouragement have been the bedrock upon which this project stands. Your endurance through countless sleepless nights and your belief in me has been the guiding force that motivated me to finish this autobiography. I am forever thankful for your love and patience.

To Dominic, my front cover designer, your artistic vision and creativity have given this book a face that truly represents its essence. Thank you for your dedication and for bringing my ideas to life in such a spectacular way. Barry, my photographer, your ability to capture moments and emotions through your lens has added a vivid dimension to this book. To Shaun Hand, my diligent editor, your meticulous attention to detail and insightful feedback have been invaluable. Your expertise has refined and polished my words, ensuring that my story is told with clarity and impact. Thank you for your commitment and hard work.

I also wish to acknowledge the many different and interesting people who fill the pages of this book. Each of you has played a part in shaping my life, intertwining your stories with mine and influencing the person I've become. Additionally, to those who may not be explicitly mentioned but have played a role in my journey, your influence and support have not gone unnoticed. You have all helped in some way to mould my experiences and perspectives, and for that, I am eternally grateful. Thank you all for being a part of this incredible journey.

DISCLAIMER

To safeguard the confidentiality of specific individuals, certain names, dates, and locations have been changed to preserve the anonymity of the individuals and organisations involved. This is due to the sensitive nature of some contracts and locations where I have conducted operations. It is a proactive measure aimed at upholding the highest standards of confidentiality and data protection and ensuring that personal and sensitive details are not inadvertently disclosed, thereby minimising any potential security risks or breaches of privacy.

The information contained in this book and any associated insignias are not being used to imply that the book originates from, or is endorsed by MOD.

Beyond the Drop Zone

INTRODUCTION

Several years ago, I began documenting my life's experiences in writing. I wanted to unravel those stories and try to understand just how they've shaped me into the man I am today. It's been a long journey, much longer than I would have wanted, but it has brought me a level of healing and perspective that, if I'm honest, I wasn't sure I'd ever reach. This book is the sum of that journey.

It was way back in 2007 that a clinical psychologist first introduced me to the therapeutic potential of writing. It was a pivotal moment in my life. I'd returned from a deployment in Afghanistan just months before, and my life had begun spiralling dangerously out of control. Yet writing gave me a form of emotional release that alcohol and violence couldn't—however hard I drank or however self-destructive I was. It allowed me to express and release emotions related to traumatic experiences. It became a lifeline.

Writing gave me a sense of agency and control over the narrative, too. It allowed me to organise my thoughts, make sense of the madness, and gain a degree of control over my experiences. By sharing glimpses here of what I've been through, I hope I can illuminate, however vaguely, a path for others grappling with the complexities of mental health and battling their demons and inner storms. This is my unfiltered voice, a direct narrative that has spoken up when words have escaped me in person. It's a bridge connecting the unspoken to the understood, and hopefully one that connects me further to my son, my family, and close friends, some of whom have witnessed me at my absolute lowest.

We all have painful experiences, and many of us harbour painful thoughts, but all too often we try to bury them in the shadows, believing that we're alone and that no one else would understand. But that's seldom a successful long-term plan. In this context, I hope this book can be a conversation starter. It's my attempt to untangle the complexities of loss, rejection, PTSD, trauma, illness, and more when time alone fails to heal. It's my sincere offering, a gesture of masculine vulnerability, presented in the hope that understanding and connection can start breaking down the destructive wall of silence that surrounds mental health.

Finally, these pages are for those friends who didn't make it back or who succumbed to the demons and horrors of war. Their names linger in our memories, their faces remembered in faded photographs. As much as it's a form of catharsis for me, this memoir is also my way of honouring *their* untold stories and recognizing the sacrifices and struggles that they went through far from the battlefield. It's a reminder that even though they're gone, they live on in our hearts, urging us to remember and pay tribute.

May these words serve as a dressing for the wounded, a guide in the darkness, and a testament to the resilience of the human spirit.

PROLOGUE

I grip the cool, textured metal of the pistol's trigger. A rush of anticipation courses through me. My heart quickens, synchronising with the rhythmic thump of my finger against the trigger guard. The weight of the weapon in my hand feels strangely empowering, both comforting and unsettling all at once.

The dry desert air heightens my senses as I focus closely on my target and the weight of the gun in my hands. I apply gentle pressure and feel the resistance building beneath my fingertip. It's as if the trigger knows the weight of its responsibility, hesitating for a fleeting moment before surrendering to my command. The mechanical click, almost imperceptible, reverberates through my hand, reminding me of the immense power I hold in my grasp.

I squeeze the trigger, and time seems to slow down as if the world is holding its breath in anticipation. Then comes the sudden release, a forceful explosion of energy unleashed into the world. The recoil, like a sudden jolt, travels up my arms, momentarily disrupting my grip. The sound of the gunshot echoes in my ears, vibrating through my very being. It's a sharp, piercing sound that cuts through the air, leaving a memorable mark on the surrounding silence.

The bullet hurtles forward, propelled by an explosive force. A mix of exhilaration and apprehension washes over me. It's an intoxicating blend of adrenaline and awareness—the realisation that a single pull of the trigger can alter lives forever. The scent of gunpowder lingers as I take a *moment to absorb the unique sensation of both power and control, surrounded by the vast expanse of the desert.*

In that moment, I become acutely aware of the immense responsibility carried by this simple action. The trigger, once squeezed, cannot be undone. The bullet in flight cannot be recalled. It's a harsh lesson that I will learn over and over again. It is a catalyst, a gateway to a cascade of consequences. Power and fragility. Control and chaos. Life is filled with both.

I am nine years old. Amidst the vast expanse of a desolate Saudi Arabian desert, I know nothing of the horrors that lie in the freedoms of war. Nigel, a trusted associate of my father, masterfully conceals the pistol in the glove box of his pickup truck, and we make a hasty exit along the dusty trail that leads us back to the highway, leaving the secrets of the arid landscape behind.

Beyond the Drop Zone

1: ROOTS AND BEGINNINGS

"What's wrong with her?" I whimper to my sister in a soft yet brittle voice. No one ever plans to see their mum in such a state. She's sprawled on the worn, pale grey carpet, her face marked with the effects of alcohol, shaking and sputtering to herself. The pungent, damp stench of cheap vodka is overpowering as she lies there, shrieking like a tormented ghost, cursing and lashing out.

This was an all-too-familiar scene during the early years of my life, a time when I was like a sponge, absorbing new information and experiences about the world around me. I don't ever remember a time when my mother wouldn't be slumped into the armchair, her speech slurred and agitated. I don't ever remember her laughing. My sister Julie, who's 12 years my senior, vividly recalls how Mum would sit there, her frail form plagued by alcoholism, clutching a pair of gleaming stainless steel household scissors, the ones with a blood-red grip handle. Her grip on them was tight, almost possessive. She would wildly wave them around, poised to go for anyone who dared approach her.

"It's okay, Mum. We'll get you a taxi... Andrew, grab her fucking legs. I'm not having her stay here!" Julie has a temper that matches our mother's. "Get off me! Fuck off!" Mum spits her words out, the bile and

hatred obvious. I've seen her like this far more often than any 11-year-old should. Once she's drunk this much, it doesn't matter what we say or do. She'll often spend hours in these states, screaming, cursing, and throwing up. Often, she'll eventually slumber into a restless sleep, her snores like the sound of a dying pig struggling to breathe.

We struggle to navigate the small spaces between our narrow kitchen cupboards and towards the back door. The ambulance is on its way. It's not the first time I've called one for my mother, crying down a payphone at the end of the street. Every inch of her feels weighty, and I struggle to lift her swollen legs beneath my trembling arms.

It's cold outside. and I hear a sickening thud as she smashes her head off the brick wall, causing a deep cut to bleed down one side of her face. She launches a volley of abuse at the ambulance crew, who then request the police to attend. I steal a moment to absorb the flashing, chaotic brilliance of the emergency services lighting up the otherwise dark Prestatyn streets like a frenzied kaleidoscope. They eventually leave, taking Mum with them.

Such memories carry the weight of both pain and, surprisingly, nostalgia. It was a time when perhaps the last of my innocence collided with the unforgiving truths of a turbulent upbringing. The innocence I lost was not abandoned, though. Instead, it transformed into a quiet strength, a silent force that propelled me forward. It would be another 16 years before I'd set eyes on my mother again, and then the reunion was not a success.

Most kids at school appeared to live with their loving, traditional families in picturesque detached homes where mothers cooked delicious homemade food and fathers took their kids to play football every weekend. We didn't have a big family, but Julie did everything in her power for me. The absence of traditional parental figures left me with a sense of longing and confusion from a young age. I often wondered if there was something inherently wrong with me. I couldn't understand why I didn't have a 'normal' mum and dad like everyone else seemed to. I can't deny that I felt jealous when I saw those other children living in their idyllic houses, riding in nice cars, and adorned in the latest clothing and trainers. Their family gatherings and extravagant holidays were worlds apart from my own experience.

Looking back, I understand that such feelings were projections of my internal struggles, but back then, I couldn't help but resent some of them for their seemingly perfect lives. I can say with some certainty that this resentment occasionally caused some friction in some of the relationships I tried to form. It can be hard to 'fit in' as a kid when you are different in so many ways.

My sister and I shared a small, one-bedroom, ground-floor flat, a space filled with memories both unique and haunting. A local heroin addict lived upstairs. When playing outside, I would often find discarded syringes lying around. Our flat had a scent of its own that I can almost smell to this day. It was a peculiar blend of damp, decaying wood and a mix of mustiness and mildew. It created an atmosphere that clung to every corner. This was the smell of a place that had seen its share of hardship and neglect. Yet Julie, with her knack for bringing beauty to even the most unexpected places, kept it immaculately clean. She meticulously arranged wooden potpourri balls with their delicate fragrances on every windowsill, doing her best to mask the innate odour. It was a testament to her resilience and her ability to infuse a touch of grace into even the harshest of surroundings.

Before that, when I was three years old, Julie and I had been forced to relocate to Saudi Arabia after our mother abandoned us. Our father, a petrochemical engineer, lived and worked there. We moved to a Western compound on the desert outskirts of a city called Al-Jubail. It was a move that left my sister, who was only 15 at the time, to navigate the challenges of being a surrogate mother to her much younger brother. Our older brother Mark, at the tender age of 17, had already fled North Wales to pursue a career as a Royal Marines Commando. As the eldest of three siblings, he and my sister were veterans of Mum's violent outbursts and alcohol-fuelled rage.

Despite the tumultuous backdrop of our family life, I cherished our time in Saudi Arabia. The days were a blissful blur of sun-soaked adventures, running around in the scorching heat, and revelling in the vast outdoor swimming pool. The warm blue gloom of the pool was like an oasis of calm and offered a welcome respite, a sanctuary of serenity in a world that had often been anything but. I can still feel and hear the soft *squelch, squelch* as I trotted around the pool before slumping into a ball of slosh from the diving board.

The heat was fierce during the summer, hot enough to scald a lizard. Dad once demonstrated how you could fry an egg on the concrete flags outside our home. Saudi was so far away from North Wales—the searing temperatures, local traditions, and Middle Eastern customs. It was a completely different way of life. The men wore long white robes called *dishdasha,* which were always immaculately pressed and worn with a pair of loose fitting trousers called *sirwal.* The traditional headdress of a Saudi man is usually white or red-and-white check and called a *shemagh.* The women wore a *niqab* or black *abaya.*

Some mornings, before sunrise, a local minibus would provide a shuttle service into the city for a few hours, returning before the unbearable heat of the afternoon. I used to tag along with my stepmom after the call for morning prayer bellowed out from the outdoor loudspeakers, usually mounted on tall minarets. These exquisite architectural structures, often found near mosques, added a touch of grandeur to the surroundings. It was a delightful ritual, filled with anticipation and the promise of new experiences.

As dawn broke, the market would gently wake from its peaceful slumber and grow into a hive of activity. There was an explosion of stalls and street vendors, each a vivid palette of unique textures and colours, offering a profusion of goods that catered to even the most diverse of tastes. Meat vendors with their assortment of fresh cuts, spices radiating their intoxicating aromas, and vendors proudly showcasing a dazzling assortment of textiles, each competing for the spotlight. There was a certain wild, fascinating rhythm to it; swarms of people practically climbed on top of each other at the counters. At the same time, though, a calm breeze would waft through the narrow alleyways, bringing with it the tantalising scent of chicken *shawarma*. The sizzling meat on the rotisserie, marinated in turmeric, cumin, sumac, and allspice, was far more enticing than the soggy vinegar stink of Prestatyn chippy teas.

Even after Julie and I returned to North Wales, I continued to travel alone and stay with Dad in Saudi Arabia every summer. One year, in the blazing midday heat, I pedalled my sky-blue BMX bike through the compound to the video rental vendor, which was next to a convenience store and outdoor pool. The sun beat down mercilessly as I glided past the majestic date trees and the outdoor swimming pool at the centre of the concrete road. Every 30 metres, imposing speed bumps forced vehicles to slow down. Then, out of nowhere, the curb surprised me. I was catapulted off my saddle, and I crashed onto the crossbar of my bike at the roadside. I heard my groin crack. A vein had ruptured, and there was a sudden rush of searing pain as I watched the blood seep down both of my legs and collect on the ground beneath my feet.

I spent the next two weeks recovering in the city's main hospital. I was well looked after by the Filipino nurses, who gave me the only TV on the ward (although I could only watch Arabic channels). Each day, I was handed a menu and could choose whatever I desired for my lunch. I loved this, and grilled chicken and chips soon became a firm favourite.

During those early years, my dad introduced me to a unique world within another compound just 20 minutes down the highway. It housed workers primarily from Malaysia, India, Bangladesh, and the Philippines who worked on petrochemical ethylene plants. They were engineers, welders, pipefitters, and machinery operators. It was a tough existence for those workers who would spend years away from their families and send what money they made back home. One of the foremen at this compound was Jessie Benger, a 4th Dan black belt in Filipino Combat Aikido. He conducted classes two or three times a week. During the seven weeks of summer that I spent there each year, I immersed myself in relentless training, the sole Westerner and child that had ever attended the classes.

Jessie stood five-foot seven and possessed a well-built and toned physique, sculpted by years of dedicated martial arts training. His deep brown eyes exuded a calm and focused demeanour, complemented by thick eyebrows and a neatly trimmed moustache that added character to his face. Despite the loss of two fingers in an engineering accident, he carried himself with quiet confidence, having been born and raised in the Philippines but having worked in Saudi Arabia for several years. Although a man of few words, he was approachable and genuinely concerned about the personal growth of his students. He took me under his wing, and I enjoyed every moment of his teachings, even though the dojo offered no respite from the sweltering heat of Saudi Arabia's humid evenings. With the absence of air conditioning, our training sessions became gruelling. We would warm up by somersaulting over bamboo sticks onto padded mats. We would then practice specific techniques, finishing the training by engaging in sparring sessions. Each class spanned several hours and fostered an atmosphere that was intense and focused, with a strong emphasis on discipline and respect. Dad, patient and supportive, would wait outside.

During those sessions, I remember how the sweat poured from me relentlessly, just like rain falling onto the mat. I loved the intensity of it, though, and the whole experience instilled fundamental values of discipline and respect at a young age—values that have stayed with me throughout my life. Notably, at the age of 10, I even had the opportunity to spar in front of the Filipino ambassador to Saudi Arabia. The gravity of representing not just myself but also the teachings of my mentor weighed heavily on my young shoulders and left an indelible positive mark on my psyche.

Beyond the Drop Zone

My sister Julie, with her piercing blue eyes that mirrored the calm glow of the ocean, was the strongest woman my dad had ever known. Her tousled blonde perm, tightly spiralled, flowed down her sun-kissed cheek like the twilight of a summer evening. The scent of coconut suntan oil and cigarettes filled the air as she gracefully passed by his chair. At just 16 years old, she made the difficult decision to say goodbye to him and Saudi Arabia and return to North Wales, taking five-year-old me with her. We were going it alone. Her voice trembled like a broken memory as she told him, "It'll only be for a little while, right?" She knew that allowing a single tear to escape would unleash a never-ending stream. Growing up was always an uphill battle for both of us. Despite still being a child herself, Julie carried the weighty responsibility of nurturing me, a duty she often found overwhelming.

We moved back to Prestatyn, to our small council flat with one bedroom, which Julie gave to me. She slept on one of those sofa pull-out beds in the living room. If anyone came round, I was either sent to my room or out to play. In the early Nineties, the town was still celebrated as 'Sunny Prestatyn', a bustling seaside treasure with a supposedly pristine shoreline, crisp, glistening waters, and lively promenade entertainment. Yet, somehow, time appeared to stand still there. To me, it was the land that time forgot—all pockmarked, Formica-topped café tables and faded postcards in creaking racks outside tacky gift shops.

Prestatyn in those days presented itself as tranquil, a place where life unfolded at a leisurely pace and a sense of personal connection permeated every interaction. There's a comfort in knowing everyone around you, but it's a double-edged sword too, as everyone knows everyone else's business and you rarely get to experience anything new. There was a predictability to life from a young age, and consequently, many teenagers fled as soon as they'd finished their GCSEs or met a partner, wanting more from life than this increasingly run-down Welsh seaside town could offer.

One of the few escapes from the routine was to drink. Evening after evening, week after week, the same locals gathered in the same pubs, seeking solace in the company of familiar faces and conversations. They drank to wash away the misery that clung to the damp, cold air blowing in from the Irish Sea. They drank to soften the sharp edges of the tenement buildings that surrounded them, the weathered bricks silently bearing the scars of countless years. Each sip was an attempt to momentarily brighten the prospects of life itself, if only for a fleeting night, as they collectively channelled their shared despair. Whatever their reason, they drank. Friday and Saturday nights in particular offered moments of respite. After a workweek of hard graft, they could lose themselves in a cacophony of wine, beer, song, and dance.

Every time Julie embarked on a night out, I would be swiftly dispatched to my bedroom as soon as the front door slammed shut, entrusted to a parade of babysitters, ranging from well-meaning aunties to close friends and colleagues from the hair salon where my sister worked. Yet embracing the opportunity to care for myself from the off, I also relished a level of independence and autonomy few children experience. I have fond memories of trips to the nearby video rental shop, where Julie allowed me to select any film my heart desired. My choices always gravitated toward horror movies; the more violent, gory, and spine-chilling, the better! *Freddy Krueger*, *Hellraiser*, and *Chucky* ranked among my cherished favourites.

My brother Mark would visit occasionally when on leave from the Royal Marines. I could hardly contain my excitement. I would patiently wait on top of my bunk bed, right by the window, gazing out through my *Power Rangers*-themed curtains. As I peered through, I would eventually see the silhouette of a man approaching the front door. At that moment, my heart would race. "Mark's here! Mark's here!" I'd shout at the top of my young lungs, announcing his arrival with unrestrained joy. I could hear the muffled sound of his voice in the hall as I leapt off my bunkbed and dashed down the stairs. He was always very meticulous about his clothing and appearance—as if he were on show in some way. He had his own smell: a masculine burst of iced mint and cologne. Standing tall and exuding an athletic grace, he possessed broad shoulders and impeccably combed, sleek brown hair that flowed backwards with a sense of effortless style. I'd follow him into the living room while Julie went to make him a cup of tea. "Mark, Mark," I'd plead with him, excitedly jumping up and down, pulling on his arm. "Have you had any fights? Can we build a den? Tell me about the Marines!" He'd ruffle my hair and play fight with me—"Show me your guard! Keep your hands up, lad!" I'd clench my fists and hold my hands up high in a boxer pose, trying to impress him. I'd throw a few jabs, and he'd parry them away with ease.

From a young age, I'd always known that I wanted to become a soldier. I was infatuated with the idea, and I immersed myself in Mark's stories of the Royal Marines. He was my hero. He would put camouflage face paint on me and a few of my friends, and we'd dress up in 68 pattern DPM combat jackets and trousers, 58 pattern webbing, and green balaclavas, reminiscent of the British combat uniforms of the early 1980s. We would spend hours playing in the woods that surrounded our estate, building makeshift dens and pretending we were soldiers.

In the same period of our lives, Jamie, or 'Saygo' as he was known, relocated to our estate to stay with his mother. Our friendship was almost inevitable, as Saygo's mum and Julie were close. Unlike my passion for the army, I think that Saygo used to just amuse me. As our dreary years at Prestatyn High School drew to a close, he developed a longing for adventure. With a glint in his eye, he dreamed of travelling to Ibiza, aspiring to work as a summer holiday rep. He was always more captivated by the allure of romance than combat.

I, on the other hand, was completely dedicated to pursuing a future in the Parachute Regiment—the Paras. I began that journey at the age of 12 when I joined my local Army Cadets, even though the official age for enrolment was 13. I was so determined to be a part of it that I lied about how old I was and even convinced Saygo to join me for a while. During those few years with the Cadets, I didn't just show up; I threw myself into every contest and experience possible. For someone as young as I was, these were golden opportunities to shape myself and to acquire skills and attitudes that would serve me throughout life. We were taught how to navigate, decipher the contours and symbols on a map, and walk on a bearing. Then there was fieldcraft—learning various techniques and methods of surviving in the great outdoors, including camouflage and concealment. Weapon handling and marksmanship were another big part of the Cadets. It was about respect and responsibility as much as skill, and I was grateful for the training.

Then came an opportunity I couldn't pass up. I was given the chance to represent Wales at Rugby Union within the Welsh Cadets, which was both challenging and incredibly rewarding. I believed that being a Cadet was as close as I could get to the real thing—to being a soldier. Mark had given me some old British military clothing from the post-Falklands era, which I cherished along with the complete collection of the UK magazine *Combat and Survival*. My best friend Cyrus and I would eagerly pore over every issue, often skipping school to venture out into the woods, wild camp, hunt, and climb mountains. I didn't truly comprehend the realities of military life, I suppose, back then. I believed that this was it.

Cyrus and I shared a profound connection, bound by our similar backgrounds and a burning desire to become part of something bigger than ourselves. For him, it was to become a Royal Marines Commando. For me, it was to earn the coveted maroon beret of the Parachute Regiment. Just like me, Cyrus had been abandoned by his mother at a young age, who'd left him in the care of his father. Their home perched atop Princess Avenue, and they shared it with George, a loyal black Schnauzer who became an inseparable part of our adventures. Cyrus's father, consumed by work all week, unwittingly provided us with the freedom to either skip school at my flat or Cyrus's place. It was during these moments that we immersed ourselves in intricate planning, meticulously packing our backpacks. To outsiders, we were merely two 13-year-old boys gallivanting in the woods, but in our vivid imaginations, we were on an elaborate covert mission deep behind enemy lines.

When we weren't lost in the woods, we were dedicated to our training. The *Combat and Survival* magazines were a treasure trove of knowledge, outlining milestone exercises for basic training. Each of these exercises, I decided, would be transformed into a gruelling physical endurance event. Our inaugural challenge was the formidable 'Combat Edge'. We would set off from my flat and jog towards a golf course nestled beside the beach. There, we'd hoist an old wooden log the length of a telegraph pole, its ends tethered with weathered blue rope for us to hold on to. Scaling the sand dunes and reaching the beach, the challenge continued along the shore. We would make periodic stops, plunging into the sea for impromptu sets of press-ups and star jumps. This rigorous routine persisted until we reached the neighbouring village, where we'd pivot and trace our steps back. The official run was an arduous five miles, though we always tacked an extra one on for good measure. Only once Cyrus, Jay, and I had completed it within the time we'd agreed on beforehand could we proceed to the next challenge.

Another favourite was a gruelling 30-mile cycle expedition west along the North Wales coastal route to the picturesque town of Llandudno and back. I had the schedule down to an art form, leaving the flat at 7:45 am, just after Julie set out for work. In moments of daring, I'd leave before her and spy on the flat from a nearby makeshift observation shelter or a tree, waiting for her to go out. I knew that if she caught me, her wrath would be swift and unrelenting, but the allure of the training was irresistible. I had decided that I didn't want to be anything else but a soldier.

I was nine when Julie first married. I remember feeling as

though I was an inconvenience sometimes, getting in the way of their new life together. Their patience drew thin at times, and it didn't take much for me to be sent to my room or to receive a hiding. The marriage was explosive at times, and extremely physical. It's a time in my life that I often think about. They were both very young, but it had such a profound effect on me. A wave of fear would flood my system whenever I heard them screaming at each other. I always tried to stay out of the way, my small figure hunched over on my bedroom floor, curled into a tight ball with my knees drawn up to my chest; my small hands pressed over my ears, my eyes wide and glistening, darting nervously from one side to the other.

Perhaps unsurprisingly, I developed involuntary tics around that time. Blinking repetitively became a silent signal of distress. Each blink was a futile attempt to shut out the world around me, which often seemed filled with anger and hostility. And then there was the grunting—an audible expression of the tension knotted within me, and a primal sound that defied words but conveyed the stress I felt at times.

My tics were a silent companion, born out of the need to navigate a world that felt both unpredictable and perilous. In the threadbare innocence of childhood, I didn't fully grasp the weight of their significance. They were a language my young self couldn't comprehend, but they held more power over me than I ever imagined. As I grew older, they gradually decreased, but they still served as a reminder of the enduring effects of those early experiences. The blinking and grunting, once brushed off as quirks, now pointed directly to the moments that built character.

I attended Prestatyn High School, and not long after starting there, I took up boxing at a nearby club twice a week. I became hooked almost immediately, thriving on the training. Although I could walk to the club from our flat, a third class, held fortnightly at another gym just outside the town, was harder to get to because we didn't have a car. I began getting lifts with the boxing coach, Rod. In those early years, I believe boxing further shaped my character and developed my resilience and grit. The gym, a dimly lit space filled with the smell of sweat and the rhythmic thud of gloves against heavy bags, became a sanctuary from the outside world. Rod, with his salt-and-pepper hair framing a weathered face etched with lines of both laughter and hardship, became a surrogate father figure, just like Jessie had been in Saudi. His belly protruded over a well-worn leather belt, but he was extremely knowledgeable and had an innate ability to diagnose flaws in a boxer's technique with a mere glance. He seldom spoke, but his silence held a weight of wisdom from decades spent in the sport.

The training sessions were hard, yet strangely exhilarating. It was in those moments of physical limitation that I discovered a profound joy—an odd satisfaction that came from conquering pain and pushing my body beyond its perceived limits. Jumping jacks, burpees, and endless rounds of shadow boxing set the tone for what lay ahead. Rod's watchful eye ensured that no slacking went unnoticed. He demanded precision in every movement, pushing us to throw crisper jabs, move with speed, and dance around the ring as if our lives depended on it. Countless rounds of sparring, pads, and bag work. The sharp sting of leather against my face. The taste of blood in my mouth. These became the bitter ingredients of my daily training. Yet I revelled in the struggle. Each punch absorbed, every dizzying blow suffered, was a lesson in resilience. It was in those moments of adversity that I found a reservoir of strength deep within, a strength that I didn't know existed until it was demanded of me. I learned to breathe through the discomfort and to stand tall when every fibre of my being screamed for respite—to be comfortable with being uncomfortable.

I had half a dozen amateur fights, but the lessons learned through those gruelling sessions transcended the confines of the ring and permeated every aspect of my life. I became a man who faced challenges head-on, who embraced adversity as an opportunity for growth. I look back fondly on those early days of boxing and those tough training sessions. It was there that I discovered resilience was an integral part of me. I was a fighter, both in and out of the ring. Years later, I went on to box in the army for the Paras, our team winning the Army Boxing Championship two years in a row.

During moments of reflection, I realise that my childhood shaped not only my memories but also who I am. The tics I developed were a language I couldn't understand as a child, but by acknowledging them as an adult, I began to uncover the hidden, often painful narrative within me. It was a journey of self-discovery, realising that, though subdued, my past deeply influenced my identity. Amid this introspection, I have also found solace in reminiscing about the cherished moments and fond memories of my childhood—and there are some good memories. Times filled with laughter and warmth that I hold dear to my heart. Be it playing with friends, travelling to the Middle East, or simple moments of contentment, they all serve to remind me that life, just like us, is always complex and not completely fucked up.

2: THE PATH CHOSEN

"It's not easy, you know," the Army Careers Office Sergeant remarks, his gaze lifting from whatever occupied his attention to settle squarely on me. Seated across the table, his impeccable uniform showcases his rank on an epaulette sleeve. His other regimental insignia are perfectly aligned. His boots reflect light with a mirror-like shine, the toe caps smooth and flawless, devoid of scuffs or blemishes. He's every inch the dedicated, professional soldier, and I can sense the weight of his experience in the intensity of his gaze. "You're still very young," he says. "Have you ever considered the Army Foundation College? It's just a year. After that, you can start Phase Two of your Para training at Catterick."

I was impressed by the man, but not by his advice. The military history books from the 1970s, 1980s, and 1990s that I fantasised over hadn't mentioned anything about college. I wasn't interested. I wanted to be like the war heroes I'd read so much about—stories of counter-insurgency operations in the Malayan jungle, defending the Falkland Islands, or patrolling the streets of Northern Ireland. I inhaled deeply, the cold, musty air of the building almost burning the back of my throat. "No," I replied with as much conviction as I could muster, trying to match his gaze. "I want to go straight into Para Depot as early as I can." He looked at me but said nothing. It was obvious by this point that I wasn't negotiating.

I tried desperately to hide any fears and doubts I was harbouring. This was a dream I had obsessed over for so long. I wasn't going to let anyone change it.

On a chillier-than-usual morning, I stood at the threshold of a significant juncture in my life. I remember the day vividly. It was 4th August 2002, and I was 16 years and nine months old—not even old enough to buy alcohol or drive a car. I boarded a train at Prestatyn station. Most of the passengers were holidaymakers returning from further up the coast or students heading back from Bangor University, but I wasn't going home; I was escaping. My destination was the Para training depot in Catterick, North Yorkshire. There were no pangs of sadness, no tearful glances back. My future—my destiny of becoming a Para—was all I was focused on.

Towards the end of my secondary education, thoughts of the Parachute Regiment consumed me entirely. I even etched the regiment's cap badge on the back of one of my GCSE exam papers—a gesture of my unwavering commitment. During the evenings, rather than revise, I would pore over the pages of books from the late Eighties that Mark had given me. I believed that these relics would give me some kind of edge: teach me extra tips, knowledge, or insights that could mould me into a better soldier. My well-thumbed copies of *The Paras* by Theodore Rowland-Entwistle and Andy McNab's *Bravo Two Zero* were also great inspirations.

Week after week, I delved into articles covering various facets of soldiering, from camouflage and concealment to bushcraft and the nuanced vulnerabilities of individuals within a platoon or squad exposed to sniper fire. Years before "manifesting" became a social media buzzword, I would scribble down page after page of self-affirmations and goals. This wasn't a passing fad or a vague dream; it wasn't even an obsession; it went beyond that. It was the very foundation of my existence, my reason for getting up every morning. At a time when my classmates were all discussing what they were going to do after their GCSEs—sixth-form, apprenticeships, jobs, the dole—I knew exactly where I was going. Into the

Paras and the hell away from Prestatyn.

Julie worked at a quaint café on the high street. We were as close as ever, but we parted ways without lengthy goodbyes or tears. She had long known and accepted that this was something I had to do. And so, in an ill-fitting navy-blue suit, and with nothing more than a duffle bag and a one-way train ticket, I set off for North Yorkshire. A change of trains at Crewe took me north-east to Darlington, where I'd been informed that a minibus would be awaiting my arrival.

Under the watchful eye of a stern and assertive corporal, Darlington train station teemed with a sea of fresh-faced, apprehensive young lads. Draped in a wet ambience that cast a dull, damp gleam on everything, North Yorkshire was noticeably colder than North Wales—no mean feat—and I clearly remember when I walked out of the station entrance how unremittingly grey the sky seemed. I stood with the other lads who'd arrived with the same purpose. Together, we awaited the minibus that would transport us to the barracks, marking the beginning of a new chapter in all of our lives.

The basic training consisted of an arduous 26-week Para Combat Infantry Course. Outside Special Forces, it's arguably the toughest selection process that the UK has to offer. It is designed to find only those who have the right attributes and qualities to serve in one of three high-readiness battalions, ready to be the first to deploy anywhere in the world at a moment's notice. There were 50 of us in the platoon. Recruits came from all over the world, including New Zealand, Australia, and South Africa. I was the youngest, something the instructors would often remind me of, saying things like, "I have holes in my t-shirt older than you, Williams."

Corporal Si King had served over 10 years in the Paras and would be our training instructor along with three other corporals, a platoon sergeant, and an officer. Corporal King was stocky and compact. He had bright, dark eyes and an almost cruel face, hardened by events. The first time we encountered him, it was hard to tell if he was smiling or scowling at us. "Joe, from now on, you will address me as

Corporal," he barked. Joe, aka Joe Crow, is a derogatory term used in the Paras to routinely berate recruits. It was the collective name we would all identify with for the next five months.

The accommodation consisted of large, eight-person dormitories. Our sleeping space consisted of a metal bed, a locker, and a kit bag. The vintage wool military blankets we were issued with needed to be folded with impeccable hospital corners so that the creases were neat and it was harder for the sheet to come untucked. This would be the place that we would call home for the next 26 weeks before moving on to the four-week Basic Parachute Course at Brize Norton. One of the lads in my room was Norwegian and could speak four languages. He came across as well-educated, and although a very capable individual, he got injured at the very end of training. I learned years later that he had been thrown in prison in Africa, accused of murder, and was possibly facing the death sentence.

The instructors were ruthless about the smallest things. At random times, we would be screamed at to line up in the corridor and 'number off'. This meant the first man in the line would scream, "One!" The next recruit, "Two!", and so on, all the way to the end of the line. If anyone messed up, we would be physically punished, usually through press-ups and other exercises. Then we would start again until it was perfect. At any time, our water bottles could be inspected, day or night, to ensure that they were full to the top. If one water bottle was even a tablespoon short, that person would be made to pour the entire contents of the bottle over their head, and we would all be punished. Then we would start again.

Even something as straightforward as eating became a challenge during basic training. Once again, we would line up in the corridor. The instructors would say, "Right, Joe. You have exactly 13 minutes to eat and be back in this corridor lined up, or fucking stand by!" Then the stopwatch would begin. One recruit being even a second late would mean everyone collectively being punished. It was impossible to do, which was the whole point. The queue in the canteen, or 'scoff house' as it's referred to in the Paras, took more than 10 minutes alone because other units used it too. I would push in at the front of the queue, despite the inevitable complaints and abuse that would erupt behind me. My lunch would be piled onto a plate. I would stuff whatever it was between two slices of bread, scrunch it into a ball shape between the palms of my hands, shove it into the map-pocket of my trousers, then sprint back to the corridor.

We ran everywhere and moved with a sense of urgency and purpose. To be caught walking would mean more blanket punishment. A favourite included lining up in the corridor and adopting a deep squat against the wall—a very effective stress-inducing position. An old floor buffer with a heavy, cast-iron head would be passed along the line with extended arms from one recruit to the next, the buffers traversing a human chain. Maintaining a strict position was paramount. If anyone was seen slacking or if the buffer touched the floor, it meant we all had to sprint around the barracks. Not only that but the last five recruits back would also be made to repeat the ordeal. Only when the instructors were satisfied would the physical thrashing end.

This might all sound pointless and cruel to outsiders, little more than sadistic bullying on the instructors' part, but those experiences were invaluable for us recruits. They built strong character, resilience, and a growth mindset. I came away from the process with self-belief that bordered on arrogance. Even the most seemingly trivial chores imparted lessons. From ironing and boot polishing to bed-making and cleaning, we bounded through adversity as a group, evolving from a random bunch of nervy young lads into a tight, highly motivated, self-disciplined, and adaptable band of soldiers.

Amidst those hardships, I also found a peculiar kind of joy. The instructors, though harsh, knew the standard required to serve in one of the three battalions. They focused on doing the basics well. The lessons they taught had been handed down from those who'd gone before us, from the formation of the Regiment during the Second World War to its then-most recent deployments in Sierra Leone, Kosovo, and the Falklands. Every challenge, no matter how gruelling, had its purpose and became a source of fulfilment.

At times, however, the instructors' lessons could reach new levels of harshness. Once, during a firing range exercise, I failed to sufficiently lubricate my weapon with oil, causing it to stop firing and a round to 'jam' in the chamber. One of the instructors raised his boot and slammed it down onto the back of my helmet, causing me to bite down on the top of my rifle's iron sight and lose a tooth. On another occasion, a member of the platoon from New Zealand started to fall asleep during an ambush due to chronic fatigue and exhaustion—we'd been awake for 48 hours straight. One of the instructors noticed him kneeling down and nodding off at a distance. He marched over and put him to sleep properly, knocking the poor lad unconscious with a right-hook to the jaw. Such brutality was what we'd signed up for, though, and we very quickly learned the importance of self-discipline and maintaining your weapon system.

The final phase of the training involved the completion of the infamous 'P Company'. P Company test events for the Parachute Regiment are an arduous series of physical and mental challenges strategically designed to evaluate a candidate's physical fitness, mental resilience, and determination. Recruits undertake Test Week during the 21st week of their Combined Infantry Course (CIC) at Catterick. Of those recruits, more than half fail. It consists of eight distinct events spread over five days and is widely recognised for its formidable difficulty. Seven events are scored, while one, the Trainasium, is a straight pass or fail. If you can't match the required level of self-discipline and motivation throughout Test Week, you're out.

Here's a brief description of some of the key P Company test events that we endured:

Milling

    Unique to the Parachute Regiment, milling sets candidates against opponents of similar height and weight, creating an unconventional but intense test of grit, aggression, and courage. Unlike traditional boxing, it involves 60 seconds of 'controlled physical aggression'. Seated on weathered gymnasium benches, candidates form a hollow square, their role being to shove fighters back into the centre if they stray beyond the makeshift ring or, if necessary, to physically hold them up. Under the watchful eyes of the directing staff, red mats define the arena.

    A long row of determined candidates lines the corridor. The nervous energy is palpable. Before entering the gym, we face off, staring into each other's eyes and screaming. The air pulsates with anticipation. As the youngest recruit in the platoon, I'm made to fight the oldest, 28-year-old Jeff Jenner.
    Once inside the gym, we're summoned to the centre of the makeshift ring and handed 12-ounce boxing gloves. Guarding or weaving punches is prohibited; instead, we're to deliver hard, straight punches without taking a foot backwards. The referee is poised with the whistle. Time seems suspended. The atmosphere is so heavy that you can physically feel it.
    The whistle blows. Leading with a barrage of straight punches, the impact of each one audible, I clench hard on my gum shield and press on. Despite being bruised and battered, Jeff is showing relentless determination, rising after each fall. He's visibly hurt—his nose is bleeding—but weirdly, that only makes me want to batter him harder. In my mind, he's got my points, and points mean prizes—in this instance, the coveted maroon beret of the Parachute Regiment. I launch another vicious assault, prompting the officer in command to call an end to the bout. My hand is raised. I've won.

(Jeff went on to have a distinguished career in 1 PARA. He was an immensely fit and dedicated Para who unfortunately died from cancer in 2012.)

10-Mile Speed March

This is conducted as a platoon, over undulating terrain, with each candidate carrying a Bergen weighing 35 lbs (plus water) and a weapon. The speed march, or TAB (Tactical Approach to Battle) as it is referred to in the Paras, must be completed in under 1 hour, 50 minutes.

Trainasium

This is a 60-foot-high aerial obstacle course designed to test upper-body strength and agility. In order to assess suitability for military parachuting, candidates must navigate a series of challenging obstacles, including rope climbs, monkey bars, and ropes at a height above ground level. This event is a straight pass or fail.

Log Race

A team event with eight candidates, each wearing a helmet and webbing, carries a 60-kg log over a distance of 1.9 miles of undulating terrain. Points are awarded for determination, aggression, and leadership skills. The log race is notably one of the hardest events, and it is not unusual for some recruits to pass out or collapse.

Steeplechase

An individual test with candidates running against the clock over a two-mile cross-country course. The course features a number of water obstacles, and having completed the cross-country element, candidates must negotiate an assault course to complete the test. The course must be completed in 19 minutes or less whilst wearing a helmet and boots.

Two-Mile Speed March

The two-mile march is conducted over Catterick Training Area, with each individual carrying a Bergen weighing 35 lbs (plus water) and a weapon. A helmet and combat jacket are also worn. The event must be completed in 18 minutes or less.

20-Mile Endurance March

A 20-mile squad march is conducted over the same area as above. Again, each individual carries a Bergen weighing 35 lbs (plus water and food) and a weapon. This must be completed in under four-and-a-half hours.

Stretcher Race

Teams of 16 carry an 80-kg stretcher over a distance of five miles, wearing a helmet, webbing, and a slung weapon system. No more than four candidates can carry the stretcher at any given time. The team negotiates a demanding route that aims to replicate a casualty evacuation.

The P Company test events are specifically designed to challenge candidates both physically and mentally. Only those who display unwavering determination and exceptional aptitude are able to successfully complete them. By passing these rigorous challenges, candidates prove their readiness to join the esteemed Parachute Regiment, showcasing their dedication and commitment to becoming elite soldiers.

I successfully passed all the P Company events before proceeding to complete Exercise Dynamite Mole, which some believe surpasses the difficulty of P Company. It's a tactical five-day exercise that involves the construction of defensive positions along the Scottish border and is characterised by extensive sleep deprivation. Recruits live and fight in trenches during the defensive phase, executing platoon attacks both day and night. The conditions when I did it were incredibly harsh and challenging. Our trenches were dug into the frozen ground, offering a little shelter from the biting wind and snowfall. Staying dry, however, proved to be a constant struggle. Melting snow and sleet incessantly seeped into the trench, soaking everything inside. The cold penetrated through every layer of clothing, chilling us to the bone. With each breath, fog formed in the frigid air, and any exposed skin quickly succumbed to numbness. Throughout the nights, the digging and constant attacks persisted, and frostbite became a real concern. The combination of cold, wetness, and the ever-present threat of attack made for an extremely stressful, exhausting experience. On the third night, I was taken to the hospital with suspected hypothermia, as were two other members of my trench. I vividly recall the relentless shivering, slurred speech, and hallucinations that gripped me. After a few hours of observations, we received the all-clear and were sent straight back to our trenches to finish the exercise. It was an accumulation of all our training, as we learned to soldier and operate as a cohesive unit in the most unforgiving conditions.

My father, who had now retired to the beautiful mountains, coastlines, and picturesque vineyards of Cyprus, travelled to the UK to attend my pass-out parade. Julie, Mark, and Cyrus came too, ensuring it would be a truly memorable moment in my life. At the end of the ceremony, our platoon marched off the cold parade square in front of our friends and family, acknowledging their unwavering support with a proud salute. The Band of the Parachute Regiment played Wagner's stirring 'Ride of the Valkyries'. There was an air of pomp and tradition, but there was triumph and camaraderie too. Everything in my life had been aimed at making this moment happen, and I'd done it. I felt an immense sense of pride in what I'd achieved at such a young age.

Soon after the celebrations, I received the news that I would be joining the 3rd Battalion, the Parachute Regiment (3 PARA), which at the time was preparing to deploy to Iraq prior to the invasion in March 2003. However, since I was only 17 years old, I had to wait until my 18th birthday before I could join the deployment. In the meantime, I became part of the rear-guard, which involved staying behind, rotating through guard duty on the camp gates, and carrying out plenty of further training.

3: BATTALION LIFE

Joining one of the battalions felt like stepping into an alternate reality where the atmosphere, thick with tension and unspoken codes of conduct, carried extra weight. Those initial months were filled with a whirlwind of emotions: uncertainty, fear, and the sharp awareness of being a newcomer. Among us were a diverse array of men from tough neighbourhoods across the UK and the Commonwealth, spanning from Glasgow to London, Liverpool to Fiji, and everywhere in between. It was a melting pot of resilient, highly driven individuals. Yet there was solace in the knowledge that everyone had endured the same rigorous training. We all donned the revered maroon beret with equal pride.

The walls of the Meanee & Hyderabad Barracks in Colchester, where we were stationed, are tall and foreboding. They were originally built at the turn of the 20th century and named after a princely state of south-central India. Their colossal, sprawling footprint is a testament to the enduring legacy of Colchester's military history and spreads a substantial shadow over the Essex city.

While there's no variance in standard among the three battalions of the Parachute Regiment, their distinctions lie in their specific roles, deployments, and operational focus. By 2001, all three had been integrated into the 16 Air Assault order of battle. The 16 Air Assault Brigade is specially trained and equipped for deployment by parachute, helicopter, and air-landing. Its primary function is to maintain the Air Assault Task Force and be prepared for rapid deployment worldwide. Its soldiers are capable of executing a wide range of missions, from non-combatant evacuation operations to full-scale warfare.

3 PARA, renowned for its illustrious history, has earned numerous operational battle honours since its establishment. Formed in September 1941, the battalion participated in pivotal parachute operations during World War 2, including engagements in Tunisia during the North African campaign, the capture of Primosole Bridge in Sicily, and the daring Operation Market Garden, where 3 PARA dropped into Arnhem, southern Holland, following the D-Day landings. The battalion had also played a crucial role in various conflicts and operations since, such as the Suez crisis, counter-insurgency campaigns in the Radfan Mountains north of Aden, and the Falklands conflict. I was assigned to 4 Platoon, B Company, 3 PARA, the same company as Sergeant Ian MacKay, who was posthumously awarded the Victoria Cross for his heroic actions during the attack on Mount Longdon in the Falklands in 1982.

As a newcomer, the hierarchy within the platoon was unmistakable, and seeking acceptance could be a daunting challenge. The gazes of the more seasoned Paras seemed to examine us with a blend of curiosity and, at times, intimidation. The acknowledged understanding was that you had to walk a tightrope—you had to assert yourself without provoking unnecessary conflict, and you had to prove your self-worth. This involved undertaking all manner of menial tasks, which served as a rite of passage and proved your willingness to conform to the battalion's unwritten code. You were the first to volunteer for anything, and you were expected to be the first one up in the morning, taking the lead on all cleaning and chores.

To ask for permission became a necessity, a gesture to

acknowledge the established order within the platoon. Every action, no matter how trivial, needed the approval of the senior private soldiers, or 'Toms' as they're known. Some of them had 10 years' experience and had firmly established their dominance in this strange social hierarchy. We had to ask their permission if we wanted to wear any non-issued personal kit, such as smocks or more comfortable boots. We had to ask what, if any, bars we were allowed to drink in around Colchester.

The highest standards were expected. The consequences of not meeting those standards could be severe, from platoon-initiated 'kangaroo courts' to 'shelling', which involved parading in front of the guard room in your No. 2 dress—khaki jacket, shirt, tie, trousers, and highly polished boots. During this punishment, you would be instructed to pick up a 60-lb brass artillery shell. The Provost Sergeant, responsible for maintaining good order and discipline within the battalion, would then subject you to a physical 'beasting' around the camp for the next few hours. This involved tasks such as sprinting, lifting, squatting, and pressing the artillery shell until the punishment was deemed satisfactory—usually when you threw up or passed out.

Initiation rituals were also common practice among the newer Toms. These rituals were diverse in nature and included fist fights with desert boots for boxing gloves, swigging down urine, and other twisted drinking games that often involved new recruits ending up naked. Taking part in those initiations, however outrageous they got, was a traditional step willingly embraced by every junior Para and part of the very reason that our brotherhood stands so robust. Through these seemingly trivial and absurd rites, we forged bonds of rapport, trust, and courage. I can appreciate that they might seem nonsensical, maybe even perverse to the uninitiated, but like our treatment by the instructors at Catterick, they weaved us into a tightly-knit, high-performing unit that could face any challenge, deployment, or operation head-on.

The distinctive roar of the C-130 Hercules aircraft, a 'Herc', punctuates the air. A primary tactical transport aircraft favoured by the RAF, it's an impressive piece of engineering used all over the world. It can carry up to 64 fully equipped paratroopers who can jump simultaneously from double doors on either side of the fuselage.

Inside, the noise is a symphony of mechanical hums, low-frequency vibrations, and the occasional sharp clatter of metal. The powerful engines create a constant background drone that permeates the entire cabin. We all stand up, check our equipment, and face the double doors in one long line. The standard British military low-level parachute (LLP) is used for static line parachute drops, including mass tactical drops of paratroopers, down to as low as 250 feet. I also have a chest-mounted reserve chute that can be deployed if the main one fails. I check that the yellow 'strop-and-snap' hook is securely connected to the aircraft anchor cable.

"Six mins!" The jump master at the front of the aircraft cries out, reinforcing his words with a hand gesture. The message is repeated all the way down the aircraft.

The green landscape below rushes by in a blur, but details become discernible. It's a unique perspective, revealing a patchwork of fields, roads, and structures. The terrain appears both vast and detailed, with the contours of the landscape becoming apparent. The moment arrives when the first para is in the doorway and the command "Red on!" is given. The jump lights serve as crucial signals for paratroopers preparing to execute a jump. The red light indicates that the aircraft is approaching the drop zone, signalling the paratroopers to stand by and prepare for the jump. "Green on! Go-o!!" The red light turns green, signifying the optimal moment for the paratroopers to exit the aircraft and execute their jump.

As I leap out, the slipstream catches me and throws me to the side of the aircraft like a rag doll. The roar of the wind and the sensation of freefalling engulf the senses. I stay tight, feet and legs pressed together and both arms folded, resting on top of my reserve chute. "One thousand, two thousand, three thousand, check canopy!" I scream, looking upwards to check that my canopy has fully opened. It's a thrilling, almost surreal experience as the world below rapidly transforms into a canvas of landscapes and the wind becomes a powerful force, propelling the descent. The ground seems like it's rushing up to meet me, and my adrenaline surges with the anticipation of landing. Thankfully, the parachute slows the descent, and there's a moment of suspension before my feet make contact with the ground. The impact sends a jolt through my entire body, and I tumble into a parachute roll in an attempt to absorb the impact of my landing. I take a moment to lie motionless on the ground and feel both invigorated and relieved to still be in one piece.

The Basic Parachute Course (BPC) at Brize Norton in Oxfordshire spanned four weeks, during which we junior Paras were taught exit, flight, and landing techniques. To earn our 'wings'—to wear the British Military Parachute Wings flash on our shoulder—we were required to complete eight descents, including a night one. Inside the large aircraft hangar, featuring wide doors and expansive interior space, stood a full-scale mock-up of a Herc fuselage, where exit training took place. Here, under the guidance of RAF parachute jumping instructors (PJIs), we learned the fundamentals of exiting aircraft and mastering flight and landing techniques, both with and without equipment.

We were taught flight drills while suspended from a hangar roof in parachute harnesses on cables, mastering parachute control during descent, and executing emergency procedures. This included untwisting rigging lines, reacting to entanglements with other parachutists, and water landings. Safe landing techniques were taught using rubber mats. As proficiency increased, the jump height gradually grew. We were taught landings from various apparatus—free-flight trainers, swings, and trapezes—to simulate and practice in-flight drills. Next, we progressed to the fan trainer, where participants were harnessed to a cable wound around a drum equipped with fan blades. Here, we learned to regulate our body movements, maintain stability in mid-air, and swiftly respond to changing circumstances. Positioned near the hangar roof, we had to leap from a platform, with the rate of descent carefully controlled to simulate a parachute descent. After this, we underwent advanced training with the exit trainer, which replicated the slipstream effects experienced during actual aircraft exits. This trainer consisted of a wooden cabin situated atop girder structures, complete with doors resembling those found on Hercules aircraft. Suspended by cables in our harnesses, we jumped from the cabin, progressively descending along the cables under the watchful guidance of the PJIs.

The next phase of the course involved a parachute descent from a Skyvan at the Weston-on-the-Green drop zone. The Skyvan is a short-haul freight utility aircraft that resembles a flying shoebox. Descents are conducted from an altitude of 800 feet (244 metres) and are known as 'clean fatigue'—you jump without any extra equipment. Once you exit the Skyvan, you don't get the roar of entering the slipstream. Instead, the noise of the aircraft is replaced by the stunning silence of the open sky and the rhythmic flap of your parachute. As you descend, the world below unfolds in a stunning array of colours and shapes. As the wind rushes past, it brings with it a thrilling sense of freedom. I loved every moment of it.

We then moved on to perform an initial descent from a Herc in single groups of six, clean fatigue, from one aircraft door. We then repeated it in groups of eight. Next, we executed our third descent, jumping in simultaneous groups of six from both sides of the plane. This was followed by a clean-fatigue night descent. After that, every descent involved jumping with equipment, again beginning with groups of six, then progressing up to the entire course in simultaneous groups.

The Basic Parachute Course served as a foundational step in preparing us soldiers for airborne operations within a high-readiness battlegroup. It would enable us to respond swiftly to global challenges and enhance our capabilities in executing a wide range of missions. It was a course that not only imparted airborne skills but also cultivated a deep sense of pride and belonging among those of us who completed it.

4: THE TROUBLES

My first operational tour was to Palace Barracks, West Belfast, in 2004 to assist the Police Service of Northern Ireland (PSNI) during the marching season. The Northern Ireland marching season spans from April to August, reaching its peak on 12th July. Throughout this period, Protestant fraternal groups, particularly the Orange Order, organise parades and marches across Northern Ireland to commemorate their cultural and historical roots. Given the historical and political implications, these activities often stir intense emotions and provoke tensions between Protestant and Catholic communities, leading to sporadic incidents of sectarian violence and unrest.

The Troubles in Northern Ireland were a conflict that lasted for over three decades. They were primarily a result of tensions between two groups: the mainly Protestant Unionists (also known as Loyalists), who wanted Northern Ireland to remain part of the United Kingdom, and the mainly Catholic Nationalists (aka Republicans), who wanted to reunite it with the rest of Ireland. The roots of this enormously complex and emotive conflict can be traced back to historical divisions between Protestants and Catholics. Issues such as discrimination against Catholics in housing and employment led to civil rights marches in the late 1960s. These in turn led

Beyond the Drop Zone

to clashes with police that erupted into violence so severe that the British Army was deployed to keep the peace. They ended up staying for nearly 40 years. During the 1970s and 1980s in particular, the Troubles wrought devastation. Bombings, assassinations, shootings, and other acts of violence were carried out by paramilitary groups on both sides, as well as by the army and the police. Thousands of people, including children, were killed or injured, and some communities remain deeply divided to this day.

In the early 2000s, resentment of the British Army's presence on Northern Ireland's streets was still palpable. While the peace process had made significant progress with the Good Friday Agreement in 1998, the scars of the past ran deep, and the region remained a hotbed of political, sectarian, and paramilitary tensions. The army remained there because the situation was still, at best, volatile. Although a ceasefire had been declared by the main paramilitary groups (the Provisional Irish Republican Army (IRA) and the Combined Loyalist Military Command), splinter factions were still engaging in sporadic acts of violence. Groups such as the Nationalist 'Real IRA' and the Unionist 'Red Hand Defenders' were still using guns and bombs to terrorise, kill, and maim. They were also executing members of their own organisations amid bitter internal power struggles. This all posed a constant threat to the peace process and to British troops stationed in the region. Checkpoints, armoured vehicles, and fortified barracks were therefore a common sight, serving as a stark reminder of the ongoing security concerns.

Operation Banner was the name given to what was to become the longest continuous deployment in British military history. Between 1969 and 2007, soldiers were stationed in potential hotspots such as Londonderry, Belfast, and South Armagh. I experienced the atmosphere of simmering violence first-hand when I was stationed at Palace Barracks, West Belfast, during the operation's closing tours.

Our pre-deployment training took place in Kent, where we immersed ourselves in mock-up towns and streets meticulously crafted to replicate the urban landscape of Northern Ireland. The training regimen proved to be rigorous and immersive. We received training on an array of tactics and manoeuvres crucial for crowd control and order maintenance. From formations for advancing, holding, and withdrawing to the finer points of barricade establishment and perimeter defence, we honed our skills. We familiarised ourselves with the use of non-lethal weapons like tear gas, rubber bullets, water cannons, and batons, engaging in lifelike scenarios mirroring civil unrest, from protests to full-scale riots. It was an invaluable practical experience. These simulations served as crucibles for our decision-making abilities, ensuring we could navigate evolving situations with precision and maintain unwavering situational awareness.

We underwent petrol bombing inoculation—a vital facet of riot control training tailored to prepare us for the menace of Molotov cocktails or petrol bombs. The experience was both intense and exhilarating. Each of us stood in formation, clad in our riot gear, helmets adorned with face visors, the weighty Perspex shields adding an imposing presence. As the drills commenced, Molotov cocktails were hurled to the ground, rupturing into an immediate explosion accompanied by the distinct shattering of glass. Flames erupted with ferocity, casting a sudden and eerie illumination over our surroundings. The acrid stench of burning fuel hung heavy in the air, mingling with the chaos of glass fragments scattering in all directions like fiery confetti. Then came the urgent command: "Stamp your feet!" In a furious frenzy, I stomped vigorously, attempting to extinguish the flames that threatened to consume and burn my lower limbs.

By the 12th July, tensions had steadily risen in North Belfast as Nationalist residents voiced opposition to a Unionist parade passing through their area. The Parades Commission intervened, only permitting the Orange Order to proceed past the Nationalist Ardoyne shops and saying that any supporters following it would be stopped. This decision ignited violent clashes, but the situation was to escalate even further.

On the day, nearly 800 soldiers, including 3 PARA, were positioned around the area to assist the hundreds of riot police. More than 100,000 Orangemen, women, and children marched in commemoration of the victory of Protestant William of Orange over Catholic James II at the Battle of the Boyne in 1690, marking the culmination of the Protestant marching season. The Orange Order initially marched peacefully, followed by bands and Orange children being transported by bus. However, despite the Parades Commission's initial ruling, several hundred Unionist supporters had been permitted to walk up the road as well. They arrived saluting with two fists, waving paramilitary flags, and singing the Orange anthem, 'The Sash My Father Wore', at the top of their voices. The thousands of Nationalist protestors gathered behind the extensive police riot screens immediately turned hostile, hurling bottles, rocks, bricks, and any available objects, including uprooted trees, at the police. A vicious mob cornered some 15 soldiers, pushing them against a fence and beating them with rocks and baseball bats.

The riot was unforgettable. An atmosphere thick with adrenaline, fear, anger, and smoke. The crowds and sounds were a chaotic mix of roars, pleas, and shattered glass. It felt like a different kind of battlefield. Aged just 18, I got a chilling realisation of being in a place where death or serious injury was an immediate reality—there were people here who wanted to kill me. This reality was my constant companion as we patrolled the streets in our Snatch Land Rovers. These vehicles, endearingly known as 'mobile coffins', were lightly armoured patrol vehicles. Originally intended for low-risk patrol duties, they later found themselves in the harsh terrains of Afghanistan and Iraq.

"This is fucking madness!" Jay shouted above the noise. Jay and I had been at school together and had both joined the Paras. Despite his slight frame, Jay was an excellent featherweight boxer. His deep-set, large brown eyes held a unique intensity, and his nose bore the marks of countless sparring sessions. I nodded, tightly gripping the hickory stick used for crowd control. "Don't want to get grabbed by these fuckers," I replied, trying to sound calm as panic clutched my stomach. The crowd surged towards us, a living entity of rage. Stories I'd heard of the 1988 'Corporals' killings, where two British soldiers had strayed into an IRA funeral procession and been brutally executed in broad daylight, lingered in my mind. The aftermaths of beatings and grim tales of kneecappings had also left a lasting impression.

Petrol bombs were thrown, one after another, but we stood our ground. Our lines held strong, even when the crowd rushed the baseline, refusing to back down. It was an incredibly primal and intimate experience—unadulterated violence that could turn fatal in an instant. The hatred some had for us and what we symbolised was tangible. They'd beat any of us to a pulp without a second thought. In an attempt to control the situation, the PSNI used water cannons and plastic baton rounds to push back the rioters. The streets were chaotic, becoming paved with broken glass, bricks, and other debris as projectiles continued to be hurled. As a result of the riots, the Protestant Orange Order Whiterock parade was eventually re-routed, igniting yet more violence that spread rapidly to nearby towns. This chaos was further fuelled by the ongoing feud between members of the Ulster Volunteer Force and the Loyalist Volunteer Force, two Protestant paramilitaries supposedly on the same side.

The political landscape in Northern Ireland remained gridlocked during this period. The power-sharing government, an essential component of the Good Friday Agreement, faced recurring disputes and collapses, contributing to a sense of instability. But although there were other sporadic public order incidents, the rest of my tour remained largely uneventful. The occasional surge of adrenaline from being in action and away from the usual routines of battalion life in Colchester was refreshing. It also gave me an ideal opportunity to fully immerse myself within the platoon, enhancing the camaraderie and brotherhood among us.

During certain weekends, our forays into Belfast meant navigating its streets with a constant awareness of the invisible boundaries lurking around us. Each step carried the weight of potential danger but also held the promise of discovery in this captivating city. As young Paras, we embraced the exhilarating mix of excitement and risk, fully aware of the potential for dire consequences given our reasons for being there in the first place.

One memorable occasion saw Jay, myself, and a few other lads from the platoon venture to a bodybuilding shop for some protein powder, just beyond the imperceptible lines demarcating Belfast's no-go zones. These divisions felt as tangible as the cobblestone streets beneath our boots. It was a reminder of the silent but ever-present forbidding undertone that permeated the city. Leaving the shop, we emerged into an eerie silence that engulfed a deserted street. The abrupt closure of nearby shops on a Saturday afternoon, coupled with the unsettling presence of a man observing us from a car nearby, heightened our senses. His observation, 'dicking' as its known in the military, was enough to send a chill down our spines as we realised the potential danger we could be in. We swiftly retreated to the safety of the city centre, constantly checking for signs that we were being followed. It was a stark reminder of the precarious environment we navigated on a daily basis.

Despite our efforts to blend in, our identity as soldiers invariably set us apart. Our appearance, demeanour, and purpose were unmistakable, leaving little room for anonymity. The barracks gym was a refuge during the deployment, offering some solace amidst the chaos beyond the tall barrack walls. Within it, we found release in the repetitive motions of lifting weights and keeping fit. It provided a brief respite from the rigours of training, intelligence briefings, and patrols that consumed our days.

Reflecting on those years, I recognise the Troubles as a complicated interplay of politics, religion, and identity. It was a chapter in my life that began to mould me as a young soldier, exposing me to the raw essence of humanity in all its beauty and ugliness, shaping my perspective, and instilling within me a profound empathy for the human condition.

5: OPERATION TELIC

My first operational deployment to Iraq came in May 2005. I was sent to Basra, Iraq's second-largest city, one at the heart of the Operation Telic campaign, which remains one of the largest deployments of British forces since the Second World War. I was a fresh-faced, 19-year-old soldier at a time when Iraq was extremely challenging and volatile. This was a period marked by ongoing insurgency, sectarian violence, and instability following the US-led invasion of March 2003. At the time, Iraq also faced a significant threat from various insurgent groups, including Al-Qaeda in Iraq (AQI) and other armed factions. These groups were a very different enemy to the paramilitaries in Northern Ireland and capable of extreme violence. There were frequent car bombings, ambushes, and a very real threat from suicide bombings carried out against both military targets and civilians. Their attacks were becoming increasingly complex and effective in their execution.

Amidst the escalating violence, Basra witnessed increased indirect fire (IDF) and mortar attacks on military bases and suicide bombings targeting police stations. On 18th April 2004, Lieutenant-Colonel Matt Maer, commanding the 1st Battalion Princess of Wales's Royal Regiment, was ambushed in Al-Amarah while travelling in a Land Rover. Fortunately, he survived, but in retaliation, the British initiated an offensive. During fierce clashes throughout May and June, Private Johnson Beharry demonstrated repeated exceptional bravery and became the first living recipient of the Victoria Cross for over 30 years.

Despite a subsequent ceasefire declaration by the cleric Muqtada al-Sadr, attacks by militias and insurgents persisted, characterised by a rise in the deadly use of improvised explosive devices (IEDs)—bombs made outside the means of conventional warfare. The situation in Basra had also become more complicated thanks to political rivalries and corruption within the local government. The presence of foreign troops striving to establish stability further compounded the complexity. In January 2005, insurgents shot down an RAF Hercules, resulting in the deaths of nine airmen and one soldier. Mob attacks on UK tanks and numerous casualties from roadside bombs added to the turmoil.

The primary objective of 3 PARA's deployment was to enhance security, counter insurgency, and assist in Iraq's reconstruction efforts alongside coalition partners such as the Dutch and the US. As our C-130 Hercules touched down in Basra, my heart pounded with a mix of apprehension and adrenaline. It was that same excitement that I'd felt in Belfast, only intensified. A thirst to prove myself on the deployment overshadowed any fear. The heat in Iraq was relentless. The air was heavy with humidity, and the scorching desert sun turned the barren landscape into an oven. It was a hostile environment, devoid of mercy, and we were about to spend several months trying to navigate our way through it.

We were based at Shaibah Logistics Base (SLB), the site of the British Military Hospital and also home to Dutch, Czech, Danish, and Norwegian forces. Our accommodation consisted of large, rigid-framed modular tents. These were a gritty, pale caramel colour with a canvas material over the top. Camp-cots lined the edges of the tents where we slept. This was also my first deployment as part of the specialist Machine Gun platoon I had recently joined. The Machine Gun platoon is an element of a Parachute Regiment battalion support company, along with the Mortar and Anti-Tank platoons. We would provide battalion-level fire support with general purpose and heavy machine guns (HMGs), such as the Browning 50-calibre, mounted on either a tripod or a lightly-armoured vehicle. These are capable of firing at a rate of between 400-500 rounds per minute out to a range of up to 1,800 metres.

During one mission, we departed the relative safety of the camp and set off on one of our many atmospheric patrols. These took us through heavily mined fields to the eastern border with Iran and further south towards Umm Qasr, a port of strategic importance where heavy fighting had taken place during the early days of the invasion. Merely driving along the Iraqi highways was like traversing the aftermath of a battlefield. They were littered with the blown-up, bent, and twisted frames of vehicles. I couldn't help thinking that at any moment, we could suffer a similar fate. Each of those burnt-out shells represented up to four soldiers. Soldiers with wives, children, and families who'd met their end, like pawns in the hands of destiny, being moved across a board of perilous choices, each decision reaffirming the gravity of war's relentless march. Coalition forces had been fighting for two years, yet the whole landscape seemed to be defined by decades of war and widespread insurgency.

There was a very real threat of an ambush at every intersection and every bridge. Our vehicles, laden with equipment and supplies, were easy targets. Weapons Mount Installation Kit (WMIK) were lightly armoured Land Rovers adapted to act as reconnaissance and fire support vehicles. The rear roll bar featured a 360-degree rotating turret on a rail in which a 50-calibre machine gun could be mounted. The SAS pioneered the use of the Land Rover as a mobile weapons platform during World War 2, perfecting the art of adapting utility vehicles into long-range patrol and attack vehicles. However, they provided little to no protection against IEDs.

Beyond the Drop Zone

We press on, our hearts racing and our eyes scouring the surroundings for any indication of danger. I adopt my position as the gunner, standing on the dusty floor of the WMIK, in control of the turret-mounted heavy machine gun. A shemagh tightly wrapped around my face and Wiley-X goggles offer some relief from the relentless onslaught of desert sand and wind that seems to find its way into every orifice when on patrol.

Eventually, we arrive at a remote outpost near the Iranian border. As we traverse rural farming villages, we encounter stark evidence of profound desperation. Clusters of young children gather around our convoy, their desperate cries for water echoing through the air, "Ma', ma', mister mid fadlak. Water! Water!" Among them stands a slight, barefoot child on the weathered pavement, her eyes telling tales of enduring hardships. The innocence in her gaze sharply contrasts with the severity of her situation. She delicately pinches her tiny fingers and thumb and brings them close to her lips, a silent plea for food—a vivid and heart-rending scene against the backdrop of deprivation. I hand her a bottle of water, but a young boy quickly snatches it from her in desperation and runs away.

We touch base with Iraqi soldiers at the fortified outpost. It's a no-nonsense assembly of sand-coloured walls and watchtowers that blend with the desert environment, providing a degree of camouflage and designed to withstand the harsh elements and potential threats. Guard towers pierce the sky, strategically positioned to provide an unobstructed view of the surroundings. They act as vantage points for monitoring the border, offering a vigilant gaze over the surrounding landscape. A series of bunkers and trenches have been dug around the outpost for protection.

Our convoy of four vehicles waits at the perimeter fencing, which is topped with barbed wire. The air carries the scent of dust and sun-baked earth. The patrol commander liaises with his Iraqi counterpart at the barrier to the fort. A sudden burst of automatic weapon fire reverberates—kak-kak-kak-kak. Most rounds fly overhead, with a few striking the desert floor behind the convoy. In response, the distinctive, rhythmic sound of four Browning 50-cals "making ready"—their retracting slide handles being pulled back and then released—fills the air. A resonant click follows as a round is chambered. We're ready to fire back. I survey the far ground for a firing position. It's the first time I've ever come under fire, though we're quickly instructed not to retaliate. The Iraqi commander signals with his hand raised—palm outward, fingers slightly apart, thumb tucked in—telling us to relax and trying to defuse the tension. We're informed that these minor, provocative skirmishes often occur along the border. Random shots are fired in the general direction, but we're not directly targeted. To avoid escalation, we resume our patrol through the Iraqi desert.

Despite the high-risk environment we were operating in, I discovered an exhilarating sensation working within small, elite, self-sustaining teams. Often out in the remote Iraqi desert for days at a time, we functioned as a close-knit unit, akin to a band of brothers, each relying on the other for survival. The unwavering trust placed in every individual and the profound bond within the group were captivating. They fuelled our determination and sense of purpose.

Back at SLB, our days followed a familiar routine of early morning runs around the airbase and evening strength-training sessions. Between missions, there seemed to be an abundance of time to fill. We'd gather around those vintage portable DVD players with their seven-inch screens and flip-over lids, watching films to pass the time. Card games, reading, and writing letters home were also common pastimes. Soldiers often liken operational deployments to a cycle of prolonged monotony broken by fleeting bursts of adrenaline-fuelled excitement, and this is true. Most days are consumed by routine tasks, training sessions, and waiting periods, interrupted only by moments of combat or high-stress situations when out on the ground. But while the downtime can weigh heavily on your mind, those moments at the other end of the spectrum always remind you, sometimes harshly, that being on deployment is ultimately unpredictable. You have to maintain situational awareness and be prepared for the unknown.

In my experience, this dichotomy epitomises the challenges inherent in operational deployments. It's a constant cycle of anticipation and action, periods of tedium giving way to brief, intense bursts of activity way beyond those found in most walks of life. Yet, amidst the monotony and excitement, I came to understand that it was all part of a collective journey, a process of growth forged through shared experiences. To me, Operation Telic represented more than just combat. It was, at times, a test that shaped me into the soldier I aspired to become. At times, it involved confronting fear head-on and emerging stronger as a result. Above all, it highlighted the significant impact of war on individuals and communities, from young soldiers to the local communities we interacted with. The true cost of war, which extends far beyond the battlefield, was something that certainly made a lasting impression on my consciousness.

More broadly, Operation Telic also marked a crucial chapter in the UK's involvement in the Middle East, reflecting the multifaceted nature of modern military interventions. Unlike the battles I'd read about back in Prestatyn, military objectives were now intertwined with political, humanitarian, and reconstruction endeavours aimed at fostering post-conflict stability and security. In my view, however, the UK's military involvement in Iraq was a grave mistake with devastating consequences. The sacrifice of 179 servicemen and women, along with the deaths of tens of thousands of Iraqi civilians and the significant displacement and humanitarian crisis that followed, weigh heavily on the conscience. It's evident to me that the justifications presented at the time for launching the war—including the supposed existence of WMDs and alleged connections between Saddam Hussein and Osama bin Laden—were false. The infamous 'dodgy dossier' was manipulated, using 9/11 as a convenient pretext for selling a preconceived agenda. The decision-makers may have sought to assert dominance in the Middle East, but the resulting chaos and suffering were never part of the plan. Instead of fostering stability, the invasion plunged Iraq into a cycle of violence and unrest that persists more than 20 years later. The Coalition's involvement in Iraq can hardly be deemed a success given the lack of evidence supporting the war's rationale, the loss of innocent lives, the destabilisation of the region, and the enduring insurgency that followed. If it hasn't already, history will judge the Iraq War as a misguided intervention.

Little did I know that years later, I would return to the country, donning a different uniform, tasked with confronting a different enemy on a new mission. A new threat had emerged that was both ruthless and barbaric, one that would go on to carry out numerous terrorist attacks worldwide, causing mass casualties. Their reign of terror would instil fear in populations across the globe as they seized control over large territories, posing a significant threat to regional stability and security.

6: THE GRAVEYARD OF EMPIRES

In the spring of 2006, a significant event occurred that will forever remain vivid in the memories of the 3 PARA Battle Group, which comprised over 3,000 troops. We deployed into the heart of Helmand Province in southern Afghanistan. The objective was to introduce some stability to this notoriously turbulent region. Characterised by desolation and drought, and with few accessible roads, it stood out as one of the most lawless places on Earth at that time, tainted as it was by the pervasive influence of the deadly heroin trade.

However, our arrival in the country ultimately acted as a catalyst, sparking tensions between various factions, from the tribal warlords and opium barons who controlled the illicit poppy fields to the humble, impoverished farmers whose livelihoods were intricately linked to their cultivation. More significantly, it reignited the smouldering fury of the Taliban. Here, amidst this unforgiving terrain, young men were thrust into the fury of conflict, their innocence stripped away with an intensity not witnessed since the long-forgotten battles of the Korean War some 50 years earlier.

Despite their expulsion from power after the Allied invasion in 2001, the Taliban had re-emerged, determined to expel British and coalition forces from the region. They exhibited adaptability, cunning, tactical prowess, formidable firepower, and battlefield success. What was envisioned as a peaceful mission quickly transformed into ferocious combat for 3 PARA shortly after arriving in-country. Engagements with Taliban insurgents would often last for hours, taking place in extreme temperatures of up to 50 degrees Celsius whilst carrying heavy loads exceeding 70 pounds.

Insurgents initiated attacks on Afghan government compounds in remote towns across northern Helmand, prompting British troops to defend these critical 'district centres'. However, with only 800 soldiers deployed in the entire region at any one time and limited resources at our disposal, the strategy posed significant risks. Isolated outposts, such as the rooftop position in the Sangin Valley, were a focal point of relentless attacks. In early July 2006, I deployed as part of a section of 6 Machine Gunners and a small group of specialist Paras, including Mortar Fire Controllers (MFC). We found ourselves besieged and engaged in intense combat for over 50 days, with several hundred insurgents attempting to overrun our position.

For 10 relentless months beforehand, the 3 PARA Battle Group had been wrapped up in gruelling preparations for the upcoming deployment. Our objectives were to reignite a flicker of hope for Afghanistan, re-establish a stronghold of security and stability, and crush any resurgence of the nation as a breeding ground for global terrorists. During this pre-deployment phase, we completed training in air assaults, live firing exercises, night drills, and continuous advance-to-contact drills. We also trained in Oman, where the rugged terrain resembled that of Afghanistan—the ideal environment for testing the capabilities of our vehicles and new weapon systems. Every aspect of warfare was meticulously revisited and refined in preparation for our deployment.

I deployed to Afghanistan later than the main battalion due to a lingering hand injury, which I'd sustained during one of many alcohol-fuelled scuffles in Colchester town centre. My mother's temper could occasionally rear its ugly head; it had followed me throughout my life like a malevolent secret, clinging to me like a curse. Every so often, it would catch me off guard, especially after a few pints. My temper would flare up like a wildfire, consuming everything in its path.

Yet I was desperate to join my brothers, who were already making headlines in the media. It took a heartfelt plea and persistent persuasion from the medical officer to secure an upgrade and approve my deployment. Despite the relentless throbbing of the fractured bones in my hand, I was determined to push through the pain that had become a constant companion.

In the event, I was given only three days' notice before embarking on my journey to Helmand. I was accompanied by a cohort of new Paras who'd recently joined the Battalion. We endured a gruelling eight-hour flight to Kabul, from where a Herc transported us to the well-known Camp Bastion, situated in the heart of southern Afghanistan.

Situated over 400 miles south of Kabul in the remote region of Lashkar Gah, Helmand was a desolate landscape. The construction of Camp Bastion there remains a remarkable feat in modern British military history, as the Royal Engineers had been tasked with creating a fully functional military base in just four months. This hastily built camp soon became the home of the 3 PARA battle group. For the initial units of the battalion, it was a stark contrast to what they were accustomed to. In the early days of April 2006, the camp lacked even basic amenities, with running water available for only a few hours each day, frequent power outages, and meals consisting mainly of field rations.

One of the initial impressions that left a strong impact on me was the overwhelming amount of dust. It resembled the texture of a cement mix, and when the wind picked up, it seemed to infiltrate every crevice. Upon arrival, I underwent the mandatory three-day induction program, which included tasks such as zeroing weapons, attending lectures on rules of engagement, and acquiring basic Pashto language skills.

I was so eager to join my mates on the ground and experience some first-hand action. I felt a sense of invincibility, believing I was capable of anything. I didn't fully consider the gravity and risks of the environment I would soon be operating in. The fighting in Helmand Province took place over rugged and harsh terrain. Its mountainous regions and valleys were a world away from the streets of Northern Ireland, and the fighting had already become notorious for its ferocity and intensity. Yet this was my first opportunity to engage in conventional warfare, something every Para hopes for, and I was ready for it. I longed for something memorable to look back on, something meaningful, although hindsight would prove cautionary.

Only a handful of platoon members remained at camp, and most of those were awaiting transfer flights to Kabul for much-needed rest-and-recuperation leave. The remainder were out there, scattered across Helmand, fighting the Taliban. In the evenings, I listened intently to the war stories and experiences of those who'd been out there, feeling that familiar blend of anticipation and anxiety stirring as I thought about what lay ahead for me.

Beyond the Drop Zone

I would spend hours in the outdoor swimming pool on the compound in Al-Jubail, Saudi Arabia.

Shortly after leaving Saudi Arabia to start a new life back in N.Wales with Julie.

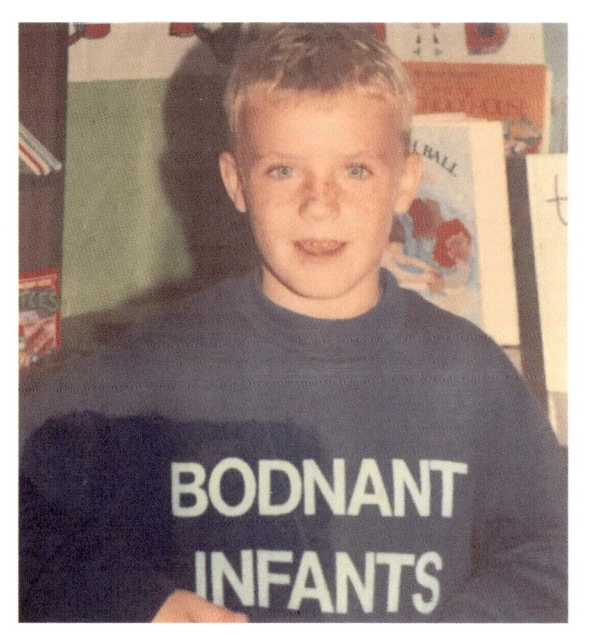

54

Beyond the Drop Zone

From a young age, I knew I wanted to become a soldier.

Eight-year-old me in Prestatyn, standing proudly beside my brother Mark, a Royal Marines Commando.

Practising Filipino Combat Aikido in Saudi Arabia. summer 1996.

Preparing for my first deployment to West Belfast, Northern Ireland, ahead of the marching season with rigorous public disorder training. Simulating the role of 'Civpop' (civilian population) during civil unrest, we face homemade missiles and petrol bombs being thrown at us.

With US Forces in Iraq, 2005. To my right are Staff Sergeant Jamie Ferguson, a combat medic who took his own life in 2020, and Company Sergeant Major Colin Beckett, who lost his life in Afghanistan in 2011.

One of many airborne exercises. This one took place in Goose Bay, Canada, in 2005 with 3 PARA.

Beyond the Drop Zone

19-year-old me during my first of many deployments to Iraq in 2005, donning the coveted maroon beret of The Parachute Regiment.

After defending a district centre from being overrun by the Taliban. The aftermath of the firefight is evident. Hundreds of spent ammunition cases are piled high beneath the GPMG tripod.

Beyond the Drop Zone

7: PLATOON HOUSE

The platoon sergeant, Mick, is a tall, lean figure with a rugged, weathered visage. He exudes a confident and authoritative air, reflecting his seasoned soldiering background. His eyes, sharp and focused, radiate a resolute determination and inner fortitude. "You're going to be part of a six-man machine gun team," he informs me.

"Where?" I ask instinctively.

"Sangin," he responds.

I'm aware that Sangin has witnessed some of the fiercest fighting to date, but I'm prepared to finally confront the enemy head-on. The task involves infiltrating into the Sangin Valley by Chinook. The CH-47 Chinook is a formidable twin-engine, tandem-rotor, heavy-lift helicopter primarily used for troop transport. It's known for its impressive versatility and durability and its ability to operate in diverse environments. We are to replace a gun group and provide fire support to A Company on the front lines in the district centre. The upcoming weeks hold the promise of unrelenting combat, allowing only brief respites from our body armour and helmets amidst ongoing enemy attacks. We will face the harsh reality of limited support, engaging fiercely in daily battles for survival.

In 2006, amidst the ongoing conflict in Afghanistan, Sangin emerged as a significant battleground within the volatile Helmand province. The town's strategic location in the Helmand Valley made it a crucial centre for opium processing and distribution, providing a lucrative source of funding for insurgent groups like the Taliban. This economic importance, coupled with Sangin's historical ties to the Taliban, intensified its role in the conflict. Under their rule, it became known as one of the most anti-Western towns in the province. The oppressive regime imposed upon its inhabitants led to widespread suffering and resistance. Those who defied the Taliban and their warlords faced brutal reprisals, including public humiliation and execution. The absence of proper infrastructure compounded the climate of fear and instability. With unpaved roads and limited access to essential services like electricity and clean water, Sangin struggled to provide even basic living conditions for its inhabitants. This environment of neglect and deprivation fuelled resentment towards both the Taliban and the Afghan government, further complicating conflict dynamics in the region.

Helmand Province had already seen a surge in violence. Alongside Sangin, towns like Musa Qaleh, Gereshk, and Now Zad also became familiar battlegrounds in the broader conflict. The Taliban's relentless attacks on government district centres prompted increased military intervention, including the deployment of paratroopers who became engaged in heavy fighting in an effort to maintain control and stability.

As the sun rose on 26th July, we boarded an early morning airlift in an attempt to avoid the watchful eyes of the Taliban below. With meticulous care, I had packed my Bergen to its limits, cramming in every last morsel of sustenance and every precious bit of ammunition it could hold. Once our boots hit the ground, the idea of a resupply anytime soon seemed very unlikely. Our only recourse was to stand firm and defend the compound with unwavering resolve against the relentless onslaught of the Taliban.

In the Chinook, I took my position on the fold-out, lightweight seats along the walls of the cargo bay, facing inwards towards the centre of the helicopter. The world outside blurred into a whirlwind of motion. The steady *thump*

thump of the rotors filled the air, vibrating through the metal frame of the helicopter. Through the windows, I caught glimpses of the earth below, shrinking until it became nothing but patchwork fields, split by lines of winding rivers. Stealing one last glimpse through the Chinook's open hatch at the fading lights of Camp Bastion, I wondered if I'd ever return to that now-familiar place. Nerves raced through me, but I ignored them. I knew deep down I wanted this experience, this mission. I wasn't sure what awaited me, but I eagerly embraced it.

Once we landed in Sangin district centre, the old governor's compound, located half a mile from the town centre, would become our new home. It appeared as little more than a skeletal shell of defensibility, bearing scant resemblance to a fortified stronghold. Some among the Machine Gun crew, seasoned veterans of previous visits to Sangin, exuded an eerie calmness—a chilling testament to the horrors they had already endured. Despite my racing heart, I was determined to mask any signs of apprehension I was beginning to feel at this point. By clenching my teeth together and controlling my breathing, I was able to maintain a composed exterior.

Traditional buildings in Helmand were commonly mud-brick in construction—a mixture of sand, clay, and straw, the bricks being sun-dried and providing insulation against the region's extreme temperatures. Traditional Afghan architecture places a strong emphasis on practicality and responding to the harsh environment. The safe house I was posted to was no different. It was built around a central courtyard, a design that promotes natural ventilation during the excruciating summer heat. It had been constructed with a specific focus on security due to the country's history of conflict and instability. The outer perimeter was made of hesco bastion—a large, collapsible wire-mesh container and heavy-duty fabric liner filled with sand and gravel. This is used as a blast wall against small-arms fire and/or explosives. The rear of the compound backed on to the river. It featured a flat roof, which we soon came to realise would be the target of many 107-mm Chinese Rocket attacks. The whole place was derelict—modern amenities such as electricity, plumbing, and heating were absent. It had been home to a significant number of Taliban and foreign fighters, and it wasn't long until I got some of the action I had been so desperate for.

On 21st June, A Company, 3 PARA assumed control over Sangin after the Taliban killed five civilians, whom they accused of collaborating with the government. A further 27 were killed shortly after when relatives of the five went to retrieve the bodies.

On the morning of 27th July, amidst a cool Afghan breeze, we're told that we will provide fire support for a foot patrol that is going into the centre of the main bazaar. The aim of such patrols is often to dominate the ground and show British and coalition forces presence to the Afghan people. One of our routine foot patrols leaves the fortified outer perimeter gates of the compound at 09:30, led by Corporal Bryan Budd, VC. I provide cover with a .50-calibre Browning machine gun, an extremely versatile weapon that's as powerful as it is reliable.

Within minutes of leaving the gate, the patrol is ambushed by a heavy number of Taliban fighters. Corporal Budd's section locates and engages two enemy gunmen on the roof of a building in central Sangin. Suddenly, two members of the patrol take a devastating hit. One of them, Danny, is severely injured, a bullet piercing his femur, fracturing the bone, and severing his femoral artery. He collapses on the open ground, exposed to enemy fire, bullets splintering the ground around him. The enemy must be driven back so that we can facilitate the evacuation of casualties. Braving the onslaught of bullets, Corporal Budd personally leads the attack on the building from which the most intense enemy fire originated. Several rocket-propelled grenades (RPGs) are fired, including 82-mm high explosive (HE) mortar bombs. The remaining fighters flee across an open field, where they are successfully engaged. Just as the dust settles, my gaze locks onto a pair of insurgents making their advance. I lay down suppressing fire. My heart is a drumbeat, my mind a whirlwind of calculated chaos.

Corporal Budd's courageous and swift action was pivotal in halting the enemy's momentum—an action undertaken at great personal risk. His bravery allowed the wounded members of his section to be safely evacuated and receive life-saving treatment.

A twisted kind of curiosity had always gnawed at me. How would I respond under fire? It's a dark truth that every soldier hopes for that moment to arrive—when they can finally put all of their training and preparation to the test. As that crucial moment unfolded for me, my nerves remained steady, defying the expected onslaught of crippling fear. There was a steely resolve, a calm amidst the chaos, as if my essence were tempered in the heat of battle. Adrenaline coursed through my veins like a raging river, infusing my senses with heightened awareness and primal urgency. When you're in a firefight, it feels as if time itself has taken on a different dimension. It seems to dilate, stretching moments into slow motion, allowing for heightened perception and response. The world around you blurs and fragments; colours fade to muted shades, and sounds grow distant and muffled. Adrenaline floods the system, inducing tunnel vision, meaning focus narrows to the immediate threat, excluding peripheral distractions. You respond instinctively to the perceived danger.

After that first engagement with the enemy, the gravity of our situation dawned on me. What happened to Danny, a guy my age with a child on the way, could easily happen to any one of us. I had no doubt after that point that we would be fighting with absolutely everything that we had. The Taliban were a well-organised, determined enemy. It wasn't long until I adapted to my surroundings and became more proactive in my approach. We were often required to take 'warning shots' at anything and anyone believed to be suspicious. Such shots may be required in situations where a verbal challenge may not be heard, such as a vehicle approaching a checkpoint and failing to stop—a potential vehicle-borne improvised explosive device (VBIED).

Those initial 49 days spent in Sangin felt like an eternity. During that time, we found ourselves in firefights two to three times a day, with some lasting over six hours. I genuinely did not believe that I would ever leave there alive. Despite repeated assurances of relief, each promise was followed by disappointment, as we would be told, "next time". Consequently, recalling every incident is challenging. My memory is often hazy, perhaps in an attempt to suppress the trauma. Nonetheless, I've documented the most vivid recollections, those I'm unable to shake from my mind no matter how much I try.

Our sustenance came from ration packs, and the river that quenched our thirst was also where we washed. The river water we drank was purified by the Royal Engineers and had a metallic undertone to it. We soon got into a routine. Like a vessel navigating treacherous seas, this brought a sense of rhythm and familiarity to our daily lives. Bonds grew unbreakably tight with the soldiers around me, and my sole purpose in this unforgiving landscape was to keep myself and those around me alive. I was also nurturing a fiery red beard, which was something of a novelty for a soldier! Meals eventually dwindled to a single daily feast, and with each passing day, the weight of duty chiselled away at my frame. I could have recited the contents of every ration pack issued by the British Army. My favourite meal was the great 'Blighty' breakfast, consisting of powdered eggs and beans with a dash or two of Tabasco sauce on top.

What we hadn't anticipated was the Taliban's shift in tactics, and this would have devastating repercussions. Their assaults on our compound mostly followed conventional warfare patterns, employing multi-directional attacks with small arms fire and RPGs. We were occasionally successful in identifying gun groups waiting to fire. Additionally, the Taliban suffered further casualties from precision bombs dropped by F16 and A10 fighter jets. Yet they soon escalated their attacks by launching 107-mm Chinese Rockets at us daily, often from distances exceeding 2,000 metres. While the immediate threat of their machine guns and RPGs was palpable at close range, the deployment of mortars and 107-mm high-explosive fragmentation rockets proved devastating from afar. I distinctly recall a pervasive feeling of helplessness and frustration during that time. Pinpointing the source of fire was a challenging task, and survival seemed to hinge on sheer chance. Tragically, during one such assault, a rocket struck a compound wall, claiming the lives of two British soldiers and an Afghan interpreter.

The enemy remained largely unseen during their firing, and the sound of the bombs being launched was often absent. Locating and engaging a mortar team proved challenging, especially considering their daily recurrence. Fortunately, the Taliban's accuracy was poor, often resulting in wide misses or rockets falling short of their targets.

Chatter on ICOM—a radio frequency commonly utilised by the Taliban—has been intercepted. It indicates that an attack is imminent. We are 'stood to', a term that refers to a state of readiness where soldiers are prepared for immediate action, typically at dawn or dusk. All of the weapon systems in our defensive positions are manned in anticipation of an enemy onslaught. As I survey the undulating contours of the Afghan landscape, I'm struck by the profound history etched into its rugged terrain. Stark and awe-inspiring, its vast expanse embodies both beauty and harshness. Glacial rivers cascade through valleys, determinedly carving their paths, while fertile plains host carpets of saffron and poppy that sway like living art in the breeze.

Suddenly, the compound is pounded by a barrage of mortar bombs, all of which strike dangerously close to our position. One lands perilously beside a defensive sanger to our front, inflicting severe injuries on two soldiers from the Royal Irish Regiment inside. Standing alongside me is Nick, a towering figure from south London known for his dependability and experience as a seasoned machine gunner. His imposing presence commands respect. He and I peer through the large first-floor compound window, which is fortified with rows of sandbags. Suddenly, a thud resonates, and one bag tumbles to the ground below. Curious, we investigate and find a mortar bomb smoking on the dried mud floor. It's a dud round that, had it detonated, would have killed us all. Despite the gravity of the situation, we share a strange moment of grim amusement amidst the chaos.

Apart from maintaining overwatch from the rooftop and repelling Taliban assaults aimed at seizing control of the compound, our responsibilities extended to deploying gun teams to support the rifle platoons during daily routine patrols. The combat was marked by its brutality and relentlessness, as we Paras often found ourselves locked in close-quarters combat with the enemy, seeing them up close. Alongside their efforts to infiltrate suicide bombers into district centre, the Taliban adapted their tactics to include increased sniper attacks and the use of roadside bombs. Our patrols were soon being referred to as 'advances to contact', given the near certainty of encountering an ambush or some form of engagement with the Taliban.

8: THE LONGEST DAY

On 29th August 2006, we were informed that we would provide two gun teams attached to B and C Company as part of an advance-to-contact mission at first light. The objective was to aid the relief, by road, of A Company out of Sangin. Stu and I were with B Company. Stu embodied tenacity and leadership. Despite his young age, he possessed maturity and quick thinking beyond his years. By this point of the tour, I was smoking heavily. I'd always hated cigarettes and viewed smoking as a disgusting habit, but I'd taken it up weeks earlier when a foreign fighter mortar team became extremely accurate at having their 82-mm bombs land in and around the compound. Within days, I was puffing through pack after pack, foolish enough to believe that it was a way of coping with the stresses we were under and the wider horrors of war.

We found ourselves attached to the rear of 5 Platoon along with several Afghan army soldiers. They looked visibly nervous, and their unease mirrored the poor condition of their kit and equipment. Some of their rifles had damaged barrels or pieces missing and were decorated with colourful ribbons. Pictures of their loved ones were attached to the rifle butts. Their eagerness to fight, despite their seeming lack of experience, made me uneasy, but I knew some of the lads in 5 Platoon, which reassured me a little.

We left the compound gates under a breath-taking Afghan sunrise. The landscape was softly illuminated, the sky becoming a vibrant canvas of pink, orange, and gold. Recently airlifted in from Camp Bastion, B Company was a refreshing sight. They carried fresh water in their bottles—a stark contrast to our sterilised river water. Their faces were fresh and clean-shaven, and they were ready to take the fight to the enemy. As for me, I was coming off a three-hour stag duty. The previous four weeks of fighting had left me both physically and mentally exhausted. Despite my fatigue, however, my ginger beard had grown magnificently, boasting thick and vibrant shades of orange.

Sergeant Paddy Caldwell was a man of lean, muscular build with weathered features that spoke of experience. The richness of his deep brown eyes, which were always alert and subtly assessing every situation, accentuated his commanding presence. His charisma was infectious, earning him the respect and loyalty of those he worked with, and his voice carried a thick Irish accent, guaranteeing attention without the need for a raised voice. Beneath his sharp wit and dry sense of humour lay deep-rooted senses of compassion and loyalty. His voice, heavy with responsibility, informed us that we were to stay close to his side, assisting with ammunition distribution and suppressing machine gun fire as needed. It was as if the very air itself was straining under the weight of anticipation, and the oppressive heat seemed to become a tangible entity as we pressed on, burdened with the weight of our bodies and their equivalent in kit and ammunition.

From our defensive positions on the rooftop, our sangers had shielded us against the elements, providing some relief from the sun's merciless onslaught. Beyond the gates, however, as we ventured deeper into the heart of Sangin, the comforting luxury of shade vanished abruptly, like a distant desert mirage. The sun's rays intensified, growing fiercer and turning the heat into an incessant, relentless force. Yet, we pressed on. As we neared the desolate market area, known as the 'bazaar', an overwhelming sense of apprehension began to creep into my veins. I found myself dreaming of the moment I could finally shed the weight that clung to my back like a second shadow. The burden, physical and metaphorical alike, seemed on the verge of being released. An eerie quiet had swallowed Sangin, transforming its usual hum into a ghostly silence. We recognised that the streets, once vibrant with daily life, now held a hushed emptiness that was almost sinister. As we progressed deeper into the heart of the deserted market square, this unsettling quiet left me on a constant edge.

The tension fractures as incoming fire tears through the air. Dakka-dakka-dakka! The unmistakable crack and thud are an immediate reminder of impending death. My heartbeat roars like thunder as the world suddenly compresses into fragments: the acrid scent of gunpowder, the gritty taste lingering on the tongue, and the rapid percussion of gunfire reverberating through the ears.

My grip tightens around my weapon. Its weight is a reassuring anchor as we look to identify the firing point. The now-familiar mix of adrenaline and fear emerges as the bitter taste of gunpowder turns to the aluminium taste of extreme stress. Smoke lingers in my nostrils. Amid the chaos, however, my mind clears, transforming into a tactical engine: calculating trajectories, anticipating movements, and orchestrating a dance of strategy and instinct. The surge of stress hormones demands decisive action. As abruptly as it began, the gunfire dies away, and the unsettling silence resumes. I carefully look around me to check that no one has been hit. My heartbeat slowly falls back into rhythm. The world expands, colours soften, and adrenaline begins to dissipate like morning mist as the world too regains its breath.

But it was far from over. What followed was a relentless seven-hour engagement with the enemy, with us ultimately managing to drive the Taliban forces north. From the moment we entered the district centre to when we finally reached the northern exploitation line by the river, it was an unbroken stretch of fierce fighting.

Some of the younger soldiers in B Company appeared to be experiencing their first firefight, a fact that I couldn't ignore. Strangely, I found myself inadequately acknowledging the immense danger we were facing. It was as though the situation had morphed into a distressingly routine scenario, one so commonplace that I initially failed to comprehend its severity. Was I unconsciously attempting to shield myself from fear, or, overwhelmed by the chaos of the moment, was I gradually separating myself from reality? Like observing the collapse of a meticulously built sandcastle as the tide comes in, each grain slipping away into an irretrievable abyss, I felt a disconcerting sense of detachment. The familiarity of the situation seemed to blur the lines between perception and reality, leaving me grappling with conflicting emotions. In hindsight, it's clear that the mind has its own way of coping with overwhelming situations, often resorting to familiar patterns as a means of self-preservation.

I draw a deep breath, the searing heat almost singeing my nostrils as I snap out of my daze and physical exhaustion. I remind myself that we have a job to do, to fucking switch on and stay vigilant; the margins between life and death are razor-thin.

We relocate to an alleyway near the edge of our company's defensive perimeter, anxiously awaiting the arrival of our company commander. With the enemy's exact whereabouts still unclear, every shadow seems to conceal a potential threat, and I brace myself for an enemy encounter. Despite having an Afghan army soldier covering our rear, unease gnaws at me. Retreating to the cover of a mud wall, we regroup and formulate a plan for a counterattack.

Bursts of enemy fire begin slicing through the air above, accompanied by sporadic RPG launches down the alleyway. A round of the latter strikes a wall just behind us, sending fragments of hard-packed mud and dirt raining down upon us. Stu and I remain poised, awaiting orders to deliver more ammunition to the assaulting section. Suddenly, a sharp crack whizzes past my face, striking a wall before ricocheting down the alley. An enemy bullet has missed my head by inches, an unwanted reminder of the imminent danger we cannot hide from.

Paddy is waving us forward. "The lead section is pinned down under heavy fire," he tells us. "Take the ammunition and grenades. Once you're there, assault the compound with the lead section." I acknowledge the orders with a nod, fully aware that the enemy is somewhere within those compound's confines. Taking cover behind a nearby wall next to an opening, we feel the impact of single rounds striking the ground around us. A sniper has zeroed in on our position and is taking calculated shots at us. My mouth has gone painfully dry, and the cacophony of gunfire creates a deafening roar in my ears, drowning out all other sound and thought.

The order is clear: wait for air support to drop a 500 lb bomb onto the compound. Then, in a blur of calculated chaos, dash across the open ground to reach the besieged section on the perimeter, some 80 metres away. Time fractures into fleeting moments, and my thoughts race like wild stallions unleashed. Fear lingers, but it's overshadowed by a primal survival instinct that sharpens my focus to a pinpoint. Vision narrows, capturing only the essentials—enemy movements, cover options, the position of the section ahead. Colours intensify; hues of danger and survival etch themselves into my mind. Each twitch of muscle becomes a dance with death as my body reacts with instinctive grace to the symphony of violence playing out before me.

We patiently await the fast air support, looking towards the open ground. Finally, the bomb hits the compound. I get to my feet and attempt to sprint forward, but I'm violently grabbed at the back of my collar by one of the non-commissioned officers (NCOs). A burst of machine gun fire hits the ground and wall in front of us with ferocious intensity. Each round splatters against the surface, sending cascades of earth and debris flying in all directions. We remain in position, awaiting the mortar team's response to our request for fire support to be directed onto the compound. Through the crackling radio, we receive the disappointing news that fast air support is no longer an option. The mortar rounds find their mark, prompting Stu and me to sprint across the exposed terrain, ammunition in tow, until we reach the mud wall guarding the compound's entrance.

In one surreal moment of respite, a member of the section extends a hand, offering us a Haribo sweet. This gesture, simple yet profound, breaks the spell. For a second, we remember that there is life outside of this turmoil—life outside of death's immediate grasp. It seems an eternity since such a treat was last within reach.

Beyond the Drop Zone

Advancing cautiously, we initiate the complex task of clearing the compound. Intermittent bursts of automatic gunfire strike the walls, and we seek refuge in nearby irrigation ditches, utilising cover to shield ourselves from the enemy's onslaught. Room by room, we methodically clear the compound, relying on hand grenades to neutralise any threats encountered along the way. With each cleared space, we establish sentries to maintain vigilance over the area.

As I hunker down, I can hear the voices of Taliban fighters beyond the mud walls that encircle the compound. Stu proposes tossing a grenade over the barrier to flush them out. However, the potential consequences outweigh the benefits, with other members of the company dispersed throughout the area and the enemy's exact location uncertain. We are told to fix bayonets to the ends of our rifles and continue to push the Taliban north towards the river, where there is no escape and they will be fighting for their lives. Literally.

Taliban fighters sporadically rush forward, firing RPGs down the alleyways and throwing grenades over the compound walls. Two Afghan National Army soldiers are killed. I know the Taliban are close by now, patiently awaiting our next encounter with them. The scorching midday sun is beating down relentlessly, intensifying the already oppressive heat. Stu and I take advantage of a lull in the action to replenish our energy, snacking on some biscuit browns and hydrating with some warm water from our belt kit. Our objective is to occupy a building located two kilometres from our current position. But as we wait, each moment stretches into eternity. We rotate through our stag positions, anxiously awaiting the order to move.

There's no way of forgetting that we're surrounded by Taliban fighters. Every so often, the silence is shattered by the thunderous boom of RPGs being fired over our heads. As I scan the area, my eyes catch sight of a previous enemy firing position, marked by a tree. The ground beneath it bears witness to the violent clash that has just taken place—a pool of blood mingles with empty AK-47 cases, which are scattered like macabre confetti. Drag marks etch a path of desperation and survival. Pushing forward towards the building feels like a race against time, a crucial step to flush out the Taliban and secure the area. Every detail, every observation, holds significance as we navigate this treacherous landscape, acutely aware that our lives hang in the balance.

Beyond the Drop Zone

A sharp, violent jolt yanks me from the numbing embrace of my surroundings; a fractured message is crackling over the radio. The gut-wrenching revelation slams into me—a member of the company has been shot. After a fleeting moment of confusion, the message is repeated: It's Paddy. The gravity of the situation hits us all instantly. Stu and I are summoned by the platoon commander—"Gun team!" We're tasked with pushing further forward into the heart of the compound, suppressing any enemy fire, and retrieving Paddy.

Immediately, Stu and I navigate the maze of compartments within the compound to a small, flat mud roof where Paddy lies motionless. We climb up there and find a chaotic scene. We're informed by a junior Para where the suspected firing position was—across a patch of open ground that joins a small vegetation block. The world narrows to a single point, and my heartbeat thunders in my ears, each pulse a reminder that, if nothing else, I'm still alive. As the event unfolds, my surroundings take on clarity. Colours intensify, sharp edges become razor-sharp, and every sound rings with a haunting resonance. The ordinary becomes extraordinary; the mundane transforms into a tapestry of dread.

Time, once a river rushing forward, slows to a sluggish trickle. My movements become deliberate yet dreamlike. My mind scatters, and adrenaline courses through my veins, electrifying every nerve end until it's almost painful. And then, just as suddenly as it began, the grip of fear begins to loosen. Time gradually resumes its normal rhythm, although my heart is still racing. The world returns to its familiar pace as I focus on our next move.

I rapidly assess Paddy and notice that a single 7.62-mm round has passed through the base of his neck. His honey-brown eyes have faded to a watery grey, filled with a terrifying emptiness. His skin has a translucent clarity that reminds me of thin glass. His lips are loose and almost lavender in colour. So much blood, his blood, has been absorbed into his clothes and body armour. "He's dead," I think blankly. I've never seen a face so white, so lifeless, so completely limp. We begin delicately manoeuvring him from the rooftop whilst receiving bursts of automatic fire. Between the three of us, we manage it. My sleeves are now saturated in his blood. We carry him back to a position of relative safety and hand him over to the medic, who rushes to give him basic battlefield medical attention. Kneeling next to his head, I remove his helmet, look into his eyes, and tell him that he's going to be okay. Stu grabs hold of me. "Let's go!" he urges. I leave whatever trauma field dressings I've got, and we return to the roof to launch a counterattack. By this point, everyone is focused on Paddy, and we're very much left on our own apart from a few other attachments to the platoon. As we withdraw, we're ambushed from the area of a corn field to our left.

We intended to identify a firing position and kill the enemy. I remember feeling so isolated. Stu had taken command of the situation and was directing all machine guns onto the identified firing positions to aid Paddy's extraction. The company sergeant major came forward on a quad bike. On the way, his bike was hit by an RPG that, miraculously, didn't detonate. There was complete chaos, in the midst of which the Taliban seized the NDS tower, using it as a refuge for their wounded as well as for women and children. This situation made it impossible for us to assault the tower without causing civilian casualties. Additionally, a sniper perched in the tower was taking precise shots at our platoon.

We soon regrouped at a rendezvous point and decided to retreat to the remnants of a structure once known as the 'Chinese restaurant'. It was now a skeletal frame, shattered by a morning airstrike from a 1,000-lb JDAM bomb. My gaze shifted to a shallow irrigation ditch beside me, where an Afghan interpreter lay motionless, rigid with fear. I nudged Chris, one of the young B Company soldiers. "Look at him," I murmured, nodding towards the interpreter. We watched as a solitary tear trickled down his dirt-streaked face. It became apparent that he'd lost control of his bladder. We looked away.

We trudged on, lugging Paddy's day sack and belt kit. By the time we reached a desolate building two kilometres away, we were the embodiment of exhaustion—physically depleted and emotionally scarred. Once inside, we dumped our gear in a room at the back. The incoming fire was by now a distant, almost insignificant echo.

We established our defences, and I busied myself with making a brew—the mundanity of the task served as a welcome distraction from the ordeal. Sentries were posted, and we lay on the dirt floor, side by side, drifting into an uneasy sleep while sporadic bursts of machine gun fire echoed in the distance. I kneeled down and leaned a shoulder against the crumbling mud compound wall. Extreme exhaustion settled in like a heavy fog, a weight pulling at every fibre of my being. With the thunderous sounds of explosions in the distance, I had already resolved to surrender myself to my pursuer, to exhaustion, to become oblivious to the world, if only for a fleeting moment. It's a relentless force that envelops you, a suffocating shroud that blurs the boundaries between wakefulness and dreams. Your limbs feel as if they're made of lead, each step requiring a monumental effort. Thoughts crawl like molasses, each one a struggle to form, let alone process.

At this point, Paddy's blood had hardened onto my clothing, hands, and under my fingernails. We still had to retreat to the district centre. Everyone was in a heightened state of alertness throughout the journey back. We halted just outside the safe house, making eye contact with C Company across the bazaar. Enemy fire was targeting them, yet we couldn't pinpoint the source. We were highly exposed. Occasionally, an RPG would be launched at us, and I couldn't help but fear being hit after surviving thus far. We waited for what seemed like an eternity for C Company to bypass us and enter the safe house so that we could follow. Stu and I then left B Company and returned to our machine guns on the rooftop, utterly exhausted and in a state of intense shock.

Paddy survived but was paralysed from the neck down. I can't help but wonder if he might have had a better prognosis had I been a little stronger and faster. I didn't see him for over a year after he was shot. It's my understanding that he has no memory of the incident, but I've never had the courage to ask him about it.

Days after B Company returned to Camp Bastion, I found myself still wearing the same shirt, stained with Paddy's dried blood, which had hardened into a dark maroon around the edges. Eventually, I was able to reach a river to scrub them clean. It was several days before it was deemed safe enough to land a helicopter, which illustrates just how isolated we were. The prevailing sentiment was that, whether dead or wounded, we were determined to make it back.

9: AMIDST THE WHIRLWIND

Early on the morning of 12th August 2006. I'm manning the gun on stag duty when I hear people screaming that someone has been hit by an enemy sniper. I desperately scan the open ground for any indication of one but find nothing. Moments later, I see the body of Lance Corporal Sean Tansey of the Household Cavalry Regiment lying lifeless on a stretcher, blood gushing from his head. It's later revealed that he'd been repairing a damaged Scimitar tank when the improvised jack he'd been using slipped in the soft sand and subsequently crushed his skull. He died of his injuries. It's a stark reminder of the fragility of life.

The daily Taliban mortar and rocket attacks escalated to unprecedented levels of intensity during that month, pushing some to the brink of collapse. I felt like I was going to have a mental and physical breakdown at times due to the constant bombardments. I experienced a tumultuous mix of emotions, ranging from seething anger to profound disappointment and grief.

On 20th August, A Company set off on another routine foot patrol into the Sangin district centre. Corporal Bryan Budd led his section on the right forward flank of a platoon clearance patrol near the district centre. A WMIK Land Rover mounted with a .50-calibre machine gun was on the patrol's left flank.

Pushing through thick vegetation, Bryan spotted several enemy fighters approximately 30 metres in front of him. In an attempt to surprise and eliminate the enemy, he initiated a flanking manoeuvre. The patrol received ferocious incoming fire. The enemy had spotted the WMIK, and the element of surprise was lost for the entire platoon. To regain the initiative, Bryan decided to assault the enemy position. As they advanced, the section came under intense fire, incapacitating three of his men. The enemy fire continued, forcing the remaining section to take cover. Yet Bryan persisted, moving forward on his own, fully aware of the potential consequences of advancing without close support. Despite being wounded, he continued his attack, killing the enemy as he charged their position.

We heard reports of two casualties and one MIA. The radio transmission crackled through the static. A gut-wrenching sensation tore through all of us when that message came through: "Missing in action", three simple words that carried the weight of countless nightmares. Inspired by Bryan's example, however, the rest of the platoon reorganised and pressed forward with their attack, eliminating more of the enemy and forcing their withdrawal.

Harrier jets and Apache helicopters were requested to provide air support for A Company on the ground. From the rooftop, we continued to lay down suppressing fire. An hour into the fighting, I observed one of our quad bikes rushing forward into the cornfields as we continued to engage enemy positions. Moments later, the quad withdrew with two of our casualties. I spotted Bryan, who was lying motionless on the stretcher attached to its rear. Another member of his platoon, who had been shot through the shoulder, sat on the back of the stretcher. Despite clearly being severely injured, he'd supported Bryan as they'd raced over the undulating terrain, making their way back to the safe house. Tragically, we were informed of Bryan's death soon after.

We later learned that when he'd been recovered, Bryan had been surrounded by three dead Taliban fighters. He undoubtedly saved the lives of many of his fellow paratroopers. Despite his injuries, his solitary action and determination against this enemy force stand out as premeditated acts of inspirational leadership and the greatest valour, which cost him his life. What he did that day rightfully earned him the Victoria Cross. He was the epitome of a Paratrooper, and I feel honoured to have served alongside him.

On another occasion, we were attacked from four directions simultaneously, and we did our best to engage the enemy. I was the number two operator on the gun. This meant I was responsible for observing where the machine gun bursts were landing, and then testing and adjusting the fire accordingly for accuracy. Enemy rounds were slicing through the air, the deafening whistling sound they produced echoing around us. One of the rounds struck a sandbag mere inches above my head, sending a shower of sand and debris scattering around me. The firefight continued throughout the night, and we expended a significant amount of ammunition. By this point, our weapon barrels were glowing hot, and we were beginning to experience some malfunctions.

I vividly recall that just moments before the attack, I'd been preparing myself a meal in my mess tin. It consisted of a mix of the contents from a boil-in-the-bag ration pouch and some instant noodles. My preparations were abruptly interrupted by the all-too-familiar *whoosh* of a Chinese Rocket narrowly missing the building, immediately followed by a deafening barrage of machine gun fire through the windows. It was a sound to which I had grown uncomfortably accustomed.

Laurie, one of my closest friends, had recently arrived in Sangin following the relief of A Company. He'd come up to the rooftop to assist with the rotation of sentry duties. This was due to a member of the team recently leaving Sangin for some well-deserved rest and recuperation. Laurie, as tough as they come, hailed from humble beginnings and was a highly respected soldier. He had deep-set, piercing blue eyes that seemed to look right through you.

One evening, as the sun gently set behind the Afghan horizon, turning the sky from bright orange to deep red, we found ourselves under this sustained multi-directional attack. Both of us were engaging a firing point from one of the sanger windows. Under the cover of night, the muzzle flash of the enemy's weapons being fired erupted as a sudden and intense burst of light, briefly lighting up the surroundings. Suddenly, Laurie began to scream and shake his left hand vigorously. As I glanced over my left shoulder, I initially thought he had burned his hand on the hot barrel of his rifle. Upon closer inspection, however, I realised that a burst of enemy fire had hit the face of the building; a few rounds had come through the window, and one had sheared off the top of Laurie's index finger.

I left my position, pulled him back from the window, and took cover behind the wall. The tip of his finger was partially attached. I did my best to reassure him, saying, "Laurie, you're going to be fine, mate. Don't look at your hand." I took out a trauma bandage, wrapped it around his finger, and applied direct pressure. Laurie had succumbed to shock at this point and was visibly pale and clammy. His breathing rate increased, and he started to show signs of confusion.

The company medic had made his way up to the roof. I explained what had happened, and Laurie was taken down for medical treatment. I returned to the window and continued fighting. The enemy had gotten quite close to the safe house during the attack, and we were very nearly overrun, quickly running out of ammunition.

One of the things I hated most about Sangin was the mortar attacks. These started to occur around three or four weeks into our stay there. We received a message through the ICOM chatter, stating that, "Friends with barrels have come over"—in other words, the Taliban had gained a large number of foreign fighters. The next day, the mortar attacks started. They were extremely accurate and usually fired in bunches of between four and six bombs. They adopted a bracketing method for the attacks. This meant that the first mortar might land just over our heads, the trajectory would be adjusted on the mortar barrel, and the next bomb would land to our front. Each successive mortar would land closer and closer. The bombs would frequently be followed by rockets and a variety of small arms fire from AK-47s, PKM machine guns, and RPGs.

During these attacks, we'd be stood to, and the guns would be manned, observing the landscape in front of us. During one such attack, Stu and I manned one of the machine gun positions on the rooftop, looking out to the east, where the 82-mm bombs were being fired from. We were desperately scanning the far distance for any indication of a firing point. The mortars had a range of up to five kilometres, so identifying a point of origin could be extremely difficult. The first few bombs landed just over our heads, to the rear of the compound. The next one hit the ground roughly 60 metres in front of us. The fall line of the bombs had perfect accuracy.

I take out two cigarettes, light both, and pass one to Stu. Amidst this turmoil, a dread-filled silence settles over the area as a collective breath is held, waiting for the inevitable. We look around and wonder where the next bomb will land. It lands 30 metres away, directly in front of the previous mortar. I watch as the bomb hits the dried, cracked mud, sending a fiery plume of smoke and debris erupting from the point of impact and leaving a large crater in the ground. The bracketing technique means that the next bomb should land directly on top of us.

In the heart of the chaos, the air is almost visible with tension, and the distant echoes of conflict reverberate through the atmosphere. The once serene landscape has transformed into a battleground, painted with shades of destruction. Smoke dances ominously across the horizon, shrouding the sun in a veil of darkness. I imagine the mortar bomb landing at any moment. I imagine the chilling whistling sound cutting through the air, growing louder and more piercing, like the pained cry of a fox in the dead of night. I imagine the deafening explosion ripping through the air, the earth violently upturned, fragments of dirt, debris, and shrapnel hurtling outwards in all directions. I imagine the screams of terror and agony and the broken, bloodied bodies of men strewn across the ground.

Stu glances at me, his eyes mirroring my own fear. He slowly raises his hand, pointing towards the pocket near the top of his ballistic plate carrier. "My morphine is here, mate," he murmurs. I nod, indicating that mine is in the same place. Every fibre of my being screams for me to run. To abandon the gun and find safety. But we wait, like trees fast-rooted in the ground. I'm here again. My surroundings take on an eerie clarity. Colours intensify, sharp edges become razor-sharp, and every sound rings with a haunting resonance. The otherwise mundane surroundings become charged with dread. Time crawls.

But the mortar never comes.

And then, just as suddenly as it began, the grip of fear eases off. The landscape of heightened senses and clasped moments starts to flicker, like a morning dream. I'm left standing at the edge of a cliff face, my heart still racing as I'm swept back into the river of existence. the world returning to its familiar pace and form. All these years later, the experience of extreme fear and the sensation of time slowing down remain etched in my memory. They remind me that even in the depths of abject terror, I persisted, and time itself bent to my experience.

As much as I'm trying here, it's difficult to truly articulate how I felt. I don't think you can ever completely convey the experience to someone who hasn't lived through it. I'd already come so close to death on so many other occasions. We all had. It happened most days. I simply wanted to be a professional soldier and make everyone proud. Life was very cheap. I never had the opportunity to fully think about the attacks; they were so frequent and relentless. None of us had the time to reflect on our experiences until years later.

Days later, the Taliban managed to obtain a 107-mm multi-rocket launcher that fired four-to-five rockets in quick succession. Fortunately, it was only fired at us on one occasion, as one of our experienced MFCs identified the firing point and the 3 PARA mortar team dropped accurate bombs on the target, destroying it and preventing any further attacks.

Our sentry duties, known as 'stags', usually consisted of several day shifts (each an hour or two long) and three-hour night shifts. We each crafted a brew mug from the remnants of a mortar bomb container. These improvised mugs, made from hardened plastic, could hold about half a litre of brew. The mugs became canvases for our thoughts, carved with dates, locations, and tallies of days spent in particular places. They served as a tangible distraction, helping us to anchor our minds in the present and away from reminiscing. The enemy was an ever-looming shadow, their attacks escalating in proximity and complexity. Occasionally, they came within throwing distance of our hand grenades. My nights teemed with restless anticipation. I was desperate to catch them in the act. They were often faceless adversaries that haunted our days and nights. Sometimes an attack would merely be a 'shoot and scoot'—a sudden burst of rockets and a spray of automatic fire followed by the sound of their retreat.

Once, while on stag and manning the .50-calibre machine gun in the early evening, I noticed a rustle in the foliage approximately 200 metres in front. Two men, one brandishing a long-barrelled weapon that resembled an RPG, emerged from the undergrowth. My finger hugged the trigger, releasing a quick burst of three-to-five rounds. I watched as the rounds hit one of them, and he fell, almost in slow motion, a swirl of dirt and dust obscuring my view and leaving me uncertain as to whether I'd hit both of them.

Moments later, a member of the Anti-Tanks platoon, through the thermal scope of a Javelin, confirmed the presence of one body. It was the first time I knew for sure that I had taken a life. The weight of the act bore down on me, a heavy realisation that I didn't ponder much thought on. In all other firefights, with so many weapon systems engaging the enemy simultaneously, it was impossible to attribute a kill to a single firer. However, this time, the kill was unmistakably mine.

We found comfort in the small reminders of home. Each day, we meticulously updated our contact charts, documenting our engagements with the enemy. Proudly displayed on a nail hanging on the wall was a makeshift sign that read 'Dish of the Day', adorned with pictures torn from old magazines depicting all kinds of food we craved—Burger King, pizzas, and other delicacies that seemed like distant dreams.

Receiving mail from back home was a lifeline, even though some of us went weeks without any. We shared whatever goodies we did receive, knowing that the simple act of sharing brought us closer together. For one of the team, however, the arrival of a letter brought only devastation. His pregnant wife had left him for another man, shattering his spirit and leaving him even more vulnerable in this unforgiving environment we called home.

In our isolated platoon house, communication with loved ones was a luxury. We were given just 20 minutes a week to call home using the satellite phones—a precious connection to the world we'd left behind. For me, it felt like a double-edged sword. I chose to distance myself from thoughts of home, considering them a weakness that would only distract me from the task at hand. The open area next to the mortar pits was one of the only spots where the phones could get a signal. It was also an area where a significant number of enemy mortar bombs had landed. For me, writing a 'bluey' letter every couple of weeks sufficed. A bluey was a method of sending free letters from service personnel deployed on operations. It allowed me to maintain a semblance of detachment and stay focused.

On 27th August, we're involved a drawn-out firefight that spans the better part of six hours. I find myself in the bottom of the sanger when a Chinese Rocket whistles through the air, its shrill cry followed by the roar of RPGs, small arms fire, and PKM machine guns.

We retaliate, and the rounds of our heavy machine guns cut through the distorted air. Like a silent alarm, the locals have already dispersed—a tell-tale sign that an attack is imminent. There's a temporary lull in the fighting, and we're given the order to "watch and shoot".

The stillness is shattered when a burst of fire tears into the safe house. My eyes scan the marketplace, landing on a young man, a teenager possibly, with an AK-47 darting across a footbridge from right to left in the distance. "There! Reference footbridge. Fucking get him!" I squeeze the trigger, firing a burst, and then adjusting my fire until the target falls. "You fucking got him, mate!" The congratulatory laughter is a hollow sound that echoes in my ears. I feel no remorse. I feel nothing.

In that moment, as the target fell, a part of me plummeted with him. The bullets didn't merely pierce his flesh; they also penetrated the soul of the man who fired them. The echo of the gunshot was swallowed by a deafening silence within him. No cheer, no victory cry could silence the storm brewing in his heart. The realisation was subdued, yet glaringly obvious: in war, there are no victors, only casualties. Each side loses a part of itself, a part that can never be reclaimed.

Years later, I was still haunted by the sight of that young man. The echoes of gunfire and the scent of gunpowder had long since dissipated, but the image of him falling remained etched in my mind, as vivid as the day it happened. I was a prisoner of my own memories, a silent victim tormented by guilt and remorse, living in a constant state of war with myself. The philosophical adage often states that time heals all wounds, but some wounds are too profound to be healed. Some scars serve as reminders of the past, of mistakes made and lives changed. These scars were just that: haunting reminders of a war that may have ended on the battlefield but that continued to rage within me.

We were rarely attacked during the night, which meant a temporary respite from the chaos. However, when attacks did come at night, they were fierce and relentless. Firefights often extended well into the small hours, but we were fortunate to have the advantage of night vision aids, something the Taliban were well aware of. Yet, as always, the darkness remained a realm of uncertainty. The ever-present threat of being overrun cast a dark shadow over us all.

One night, those of us not on sentry duty were sprawled on the cold concrete floor of our room, seeking solace in the familiarity of our makeshift beds. These were simply short camping roll mats nestled within one-person mosquito nets, with tightly rolled shemagh scarves serving as makeshift pillows. My 5.56-mm SA80 rifle and belt-kit were always within reach. The belt-kit, a chest rig from the South African Special Forces, lay at my feet, packed with essentials like ammunition, a trauma kit, hand grenades, a personal radio, and a few other basic items. It was crucial for us to keep our gear and belongings organised, given our close quarters and the professional soldiers that we were.

The night's silence is suddenly shattered by the eruption of automatic rifle fire. The sound sends adrenaline surging through us all, wrenching us from shallow sleep. As the gunfire intensifies, we realise that this is not a routine exchange of fire. Green tracer rounds pierce the darkness, streaking through the air and impacting the walls of our room. In the ensuing chaos, I scramble to my feet, darting towards the wall where our additional gear is stored, including ballistic vests and helmets. Amid the frenzy, my helmet gets knocked off its hook, disappearing into the darkness. With enemy rounds whizzing through the windows and unable to use white light without revealing our position, I waste precious time scouring the floor for it. Finally, I abandon the search, moving to an adjacent room where one of our general-purpose machine guns (GPMG) is mounted on a tripod.

I begin engaging enemy firing positions, identifiable by the bright muzzle flashes of their weapons. Enemy rounds, marked by their distinctive crack and thump, are violently whizzing all around the platoon house, striking the walls. The deafening sound of gunfire amplifies our senses. The firefight rages on. It feels like an eternity, but in reality, it probably only lasts an hour. Exhausted but alert, we return to our concrete beds. My rest is short-lived, however, as I'm soon awakened for my turn on sentry duty.

Every week, we would ask our Afghan interpreters to purchase naan breads and cigarettes from the local market. These items were a welcome luxury, accompanying our 24-hour rations. On one particular occasion in Kajaki, however, an interpreter did not return. We later learned that the Taliban had discovered his actions and had brutally executed him.

Regardless of their outward friendliness, I could never fully trust the Afghan Security Forces. A small contingent of the Afghan National Army (ANA) resided beneath our room and would frequently steal our equipment. One of the stolen items was a C2 sight from one of our mortars—an invaluable tool for recording and relaying firing positions. They would also often toss AK-47 rounds into the burn pit below our window. As these rounds heated up, they would explode, with some shards penetrating our windows and entering our living area. They also indulged in heroin use at night, carelessly leaving the used syringes scattered on the floor.

During the day, they occasionally manned a checkpoint at the river, clearly visible from one of our sangers around 200 metres away. I once witnessed them sexually assault a young boy in a straw boathouse. He'd been attempting to shepherd his goats across the river. I was informed that this horrific act was not uncommon, especially in *bacha bazi*, a Dari term that translates as 'boy play'. This practice, which involves the selling or coercion of young boys into sexual relationships with older men, is a form of child sexual abuse and exploitation. Although both illegal and repugnant, it continues in certain regions of Afghanistan. The boys involved in bacha bazi are often groomed and dressed as women.

I found myself contemplating my own mortality every day, with a strong belief that my end would likely come in that place. During that time, I reflected extensively on the fragility of life, its meaning, and what perceptions people back home held regarding the war in which we, as young men, were deeply embroiled. In Afghanistan, life is deemed very cheap. During a stint on stag duty, a paratrooper noticed an individual with a slung weapon and some binoculars acting very suspiciously. This man was pacing in the open ground, dropping a rock every 100 metres or so, and then communicating via radio. It became clear to us that he was measuring distances to aid a potential mortar attack. Positioned approximately 500 metres away near the market, a warning shot was fired to deter him. Unfortunately, the .50-

calibre round pierced a vehicle engine block, ricocheted, and struck the man in the chest. He bled profusely, eventually slumping against a concrete pillar and succumbing to his injuries. His body lay there for over a week, visible through the scopes of our snipers. Passers-by would casually ignore the deceased man, showing no reaction.

Despite the litany of horrors that I witnessed in Sangin, I admit I sometimes find myself longing for the routine and simplicity of the life I experienced there. Everything seemed more straightforward back then. We were stripped down to the essentials: food, shelter, and survival. There were no bills or financial worries; we only had each other, and there was never a dull moment. We cherished the little things, like receiving a letter from a relative or having access to fresh water. There were moments when I thought maybe I would be better off in that safe haven. Perhaps that was all I was meant for in this world. Maybe my destiny was to meet my end there. Life felt uncomplicated, and I excelled in that environment. We were left to our own devices, isolated from the rest of the world. I didn't possess many belongings, and upon returning, I struggled to reintegrate into society or socialise.

Our supplies were now running dangerously low, and the scarcity of food became a real concern. We also grew increasingly hesitant to use the makeshift toilets provided for us. They were simply large metal barrels with a wooden plank covering the top to keep flies at bay. Periodically, a few unfortunate individuals had the task of burning them. These barrels were situated outside the safe house, a brief walk away near the river. We would don full body armour and helmets and carry our weapons down to reach them. The toilets were exposed to the scorching heat, and when the mortars began raining down on the camp, the toilets bizarrely became a popular target for the bombs. On one occasion, Dom from the Guns narrowly escaped a mortar bomb that landed not too far away whilst he was using the toilets, sending him sliding along the hard gravel floor. Similar scenarios occurred more than once. As a result, we resorted to using the empty packets of rations with the help of a buddy for waste disposal, tossing them out the window and into the burn pit.

We were told on a weekly basis that we'd be on the next flight out of Sangin, only to then be told, "Next week". Both A and C companies had already rotated back to Camp Bastion. We tried not to get too excited each time they promised us that the Guns team would be on the next flight. We eventually came to believe that we would be there until the Royal Marines relieved us in October.

One evening, while I was preparing my boil-in-the-bag meal, our section commander, Gaz, a Glaswegian and an exceptional leader, came over to me. "Listen in," he said. "There's a flight coming in tonight. As it stands, we're on it."
"Fuck off. Try again," I responded in disbelief.
"I'm not bluffing," he insisted. "Pack your kit up, and be good to go." We hurriedly gathered our belongings, still in disbelief. I genuinely couldn't believe it; I thought it was too good to be true. I was expecting someone to come and tell us the flight had been called off and that we would have to endure yet another week in Sangin.

After packing our few belongings, we adorned the walls with poems about our stay and wished the Royal Marines a merry Christmas, engaging in some light-hearted banter between cap badges. We also packed what goodies we had: old magazines, bottles of Tabasco sauce, Hexi blocks, and blankets pilfered from the Afghan Army when they'd departed. Placing them in a corner of the room, we left a short note for the incoming troops, wishing them well and happy hunting.

Our transport was scheduled for 2200 hours, so we made our way down to the helicopter landing site (HLS) with all our gear and two .50-cal guns in tow. It all happened so fast. I struggled to stand under the weight of my kit, each step feeling heavier than the last. The guns were broken down into wooden boxes, each weighing 100 kg; we each shouldered one side.

Just before the Chinook arrived, we received a message over personal role radio (PRR) warning us that the Taliban had acquired a Stinger missile. This was a surface-to-air anti-aircraft missile designed to destroy anything it hit. The news shattered any hope of a safe departure. It reaffirmed my belief that we would never leave Sangin. But despite the threat, we proceeded with the pickup, although our anxiety was palpable. I genuinely thought we would be hit by the Stinger as soon as we took off. When the Chinook landed, we rushed to the tailgate, struggling to manoeuvre the heavy boxes through the cramped space and the gaping hole in the floor. The RAF crew appeared disorganised and visibly concerned, shouting orders that fell on deaf ears.

Just a few weeks earlier, we'd endured a week without food rations, surviving on biscuits and river water, after RAF resupplies had been cancelled due to the area being deemed too high-risk for landing. On another occasion, during an attack on the compound, a pilot dropped a 500-lb bomb in the wrong location. Had it detonated, many of us would have been severely injured or worse. Thankfully, it turned out to be a dud. Essential supplies like ammunition, water, and mail were frequently cancelled. At one point, we came close to running out of ammunition. We expanded up to a thousand rounds in each engagement, but with only 200 rounds per box, we faced a critical shortage. Additionally, a faulty batch of ammunition caused blockages during attacks, forcing us to use Estonian ammunition for the guns instead.

I slowly began to fill with rage at the crew. We were all fully aware of the situation we were in, and their panic was crippling our efforts. Once seated, I confronted one of the crew members. Given everything we'd been through, the last thing we were going to tolerate was someone who'd been enjoying the comforts of Camp Bastion talking down to us and barking orders. There was a small sense of relief once we eventually lifted off, but I, for one, was still expecting a Taliban missile to be fired at any moment. They would regularly call our bluff over the net, saying, "We are firing now!", knowing that our interpreters would relay messages picked up on the ICOM chatter. Fortunately, they were bluffing on this occasion.

It was extremely dark and noisy aboard the Chinook, and it was far from a comfortable ride. The noise was deafening. The powerful engines roared to life, filling the cabin with a thunderous rumble. The sound was so intense that communication became nearly impossible without shouting. As the helicopter gained altitude, the noise only amplified, creating a cacophony of engine roar and rotor-blade whooshing that drowned out all other sounds. It was an overwhelming auditory experience that left me feeling exhilarated and slightly disoriented. I was still in disbelief that we were actually leaving. It just seemed too good to be true. I felt like something had to go wrong at any moment.

Suddenly, we violently rushed towards the ground in what felt like an emergency landing. Due to the difficulty in communicating, no messages were being passed along. I thought there was a malfunction or that we had been hit. I braced myself, reaching out and gripping the cargo netting on either side of me tightly. We were, in fact, picking up a casualty at another location just outside of Sangin, which brought me immense relief. Knowing that we were helping someone in need, even amidst the chaos, filled me with a sense of purpose. Finally, we made our way across the barren desert plain back to Camp Bastion. Nothing mattered to me anymore. Having faced death so many times, I'd developed a callous attitude towards everything. Each brush with mortality had numbed me to the point where I no longer cared about the trivialities of daily life. I never once entertained thoughts of going home; instead, I embraced each day and each hour as it came, focusing solely on the task at hand.

When we eventually reached Camp Bastion, we were met by one of the platoon sergeants from the stores to help get all our kit from the HLS to the tented accommodation. It was surreal being back there, the place I had left just a few months ago, eager to get out on the ground. I found it strange not having to permanently walk around with full body armour and a helmet on. I couldn't believe my luck when I was able to get a cold, fresh bottle of water from the fridge inside the cookhouse. We dumped our bags in the tents. Our previous bed spaces had been taken over, and nearly all our comfort kit had been tampered with or gone missing—"I don't know who's got your DVD player, mate." "I haven't seen your iPod; someone borrowed it, I think." I didn't care; I was just grateful to be back.

Most of the Battalion was engaged in heavy fighting across Helmand Province, defending the district centres against persistent Taliban assaults and other counter-insurgency operations. The soldiers back at Camp Bastion had a range of critical support roles that were essential for sustaining the battle group's combat operations. This included managing the transportation and distribution of logistical supplies to various forward operating bases and outposts, analysts and intelligence officers, communications vital for coordinating operations, and Paras like ourselves who were back to rest, recuperate, and prepare for redeployment. We were barely acknowledged as we entered the room. Everyone was clean-shaven, well-fed, lying on their camp-cots with their snacks, watching movies, and passing the time. In complete silence, we began sorting through our belongings, seeing what was missing or damaged, and slowly unpacking our kit. A senior NCO approached us and simply said, "Early start tomorrow, lads. There's plenty of graft to get on with back here. PT at 0600 hours, then crack on with the vehicles." I couldn't believe what I was hearing. Each member of our section looked at one another but didn't say anything. One of them, Marc, who had been with me on that rooftop, gestured me over, and we went to grab a brew and have a smoke.

The next morning, as instructed, we cracked on with the work that had to be done on the vehicles. We figured that at least we were back at camp and alive, even if we weren't going to get a day off. But even that comfort didn't last long. Later that day, I was told we were short of men and I would make

Beyond the Drop Zone

up part of another section that would fly out to Kajaki first thing in the morning. I didn't know what to think, to be honest. I think I just went into autopilot and began packing my kit again.

Situated at the head of the Sangin Valley and Helmand River, the Kajaki Dam was designated for reconstruction, primarily focusing on replacing a large turbine and repairing the facility. This initiative aimed to provide power to two million Afghans. Unfortunately, the pervasive intensity of the fighting meant limited opportunities for essential reconstruction work. The Kajaki Dam holds significant importance for Helmand's development, and its name plays a prominent role in both military and civilian planning, making it a strategic focal point and highly contested battleground. The dam was not only a crucial piece of infrastructure for Helmand Province but also a symbol of both the potential and the challenges faced by the region. Its presence was a lifeline for many in terms of hydropower generation and water supply. The arid landscape and rugged features with steep, rocky hills and mountains with sparse vegetation added complexity to the situation, making military operations extremely challenging.

I thought to myself that it couldn't be any worse than Sangin—and at least I would be with a few of my close mates from Support Company. I knew that there had been some intense fighting in Kajaki previously and that it was a notoriously heavily mined area, a hangover from the Soviet-Afghan War. It was also an area that would forever be associated with Corporal Mark Wright, GC and a poignant reminder of his sacrifice. Just a few weeks previously, on 6th September, Taliban militants had been observed setting up a checkpoint by sniper Lance Corporal Stewart 'Stu' Hale. He'd promptly alerted Corporal Stu Pearson, who was overseeing the Normandy outpost and had pinpointed a superior vantage point across the dam. While advancing toward it, however, a Soviet anti-personnel mine had been triggered, causing an explosion that cost Lance Corporal Hale a finger and part of his leg. He received life-saving trauma care on-site, but it became apparent to the soldiers that they were positioned in the midst of a minefield. Immediate assistance was sought from nearby units, including a U.S. Black Hawk helicopter equipped with a winch for safe evacuation in the presence of landmines. Stu was relocated to a safer spot near the river bed as additional troops arrived.

In the midst of this, though, another explosion occurred, and with another Black Hawk unavailable, a Chinook had been dispatched instead. However, the downdraft from the Chinook's blades triggered a third mine, leading to the tragic death of Corporal Wright and causing severe injuries to others who were attempting to aid the injured soldiers. Four hours after the initial explosion, two Black Hawks equipped with winches finally arrived. For his bravery, Corporal Wright was posthumously awarded the George Cross. His citation read: "Despite this horrific situation and the serious injuries he had himself sustained, Corporal Wright continued to command and control the incident. He remained conscious for the majority of the time, continually shouting encouragement to those around, maintaining morale and calm amongst the many wounded men." The incident was later adapted into the BAFTA-nominated motion picture, *Kajaki*.

We undertook a road convoy from Lashkar Gah to Kajaki, escorting a large turbine across hazardous Afghan terrain as part of a substantial convoy. The journey was expected to span more than six hours, tracing our route back through the Sangin Valley alongside the Helmand River North. Equipped with WMIK Land Rover vehicles, each armed with a .50-cal machine gun and a pintle-mount for a GPMG next to the vehicle commander, we ensured complete self-sufficiency by loading the WMIKs with supplies for several weeks ahead.

The convoy resembled a massive serpent winding through the landscape, with me assigned the task of driving one of the WMIKs. While effective for reconnaissance and fire support, its narrow wheels did pose a challenge on Afghanistan's rugged off-road terrain. Accompanying me was the platoon commander, Captain MacKenzie, who repeatedly demonstrated exceptional leadership throughout the deployment.

Departing Camp Bastion early in the morning, we headed north. Just beyond Gereshk, we encountered enemy contact on the open ground. Looking across Captain MacKenzie to my left, I identified a narrow *wadi* (a dry riverbed and valley formed over time by erosion) to the west with steep sides and a rocky floor that offered some cover from the incoming fire. The WMIK roared forward, the gunner manning the machine gun mounted atop its turret. With each squeeze of the trigger, the deafening roar echoed across the landscape as the powerful rounds tore through the air, leaving a trail of smoke in their wake. The vehicle's chassis reverberated with the force of each burst, causing it to rock on its suspension with each recoil. The gunner maintained a steady aim, unleashing bursts of suppressive fire against firing positions in the distance. Enemy rounds narrowly missed our vehicle, punctuated by the unmistakable crack and thud of their impact nearby. Adrenaline surged through us as we sought cover, feeling the vehicle shudder with the force of each near-miss. Although one of the flatbed trucks ahead of us was peppered with machine gun fire, we fortunately sustained no casualties.

In response, air support was requested, and an Apache attack helicopter swiftly arrived to aid the convoy. Positioned directly overhead, it unleashed a thunderous volley from the 30-mm M230 chain gun mounted under its forward fuselage. With a firing rate of up to 625 rounds per minute, it produced a deep, guttural roar, punctuated by sharp, rapid bursts of gunfire. The expended cartridges rained down around us, some bouncing off the bonnet of our WMIK like hailstones on a metal roof.

The convoy eventually arrived in Kajaki, and one of the first things that struck me was its breath-taking and rugged scenic views. Towering mountain ranges stretched into the distance, their jagged peaks piercing the sky. The landscape was painted with hues of earthy browns, the vibrant greens of scattered vegetation, and occasional pops of colourful wildflowers. The Helmand River wound its way through the valley below, its waters shimmering in the sunlight. In the distance, small villages dotted the terrain, their mud-brick homes blending harmoniously with the natural surroundings, capturing Afghanistan's natural beauty. Perched atop the mountain, we set up our machine gun positions. For the duration, we would sleep under a poncho or *basha*, a term long associated with the British Army. It's a sheet of lightweight camouflage tarpaulin with eyelets on the perimeter, providing us with a place to rest, sleep, and take cover from the elements while deployed on operations. Paired up with Stu, we reinforced our makeshift shelter with sandbags.

Kajaki remains one of the most heavily mined regions in the world. Well aware of the tragic events that had occurred just a few weeks prior, we kept our movements strictly to predetermined paths. In between rotating through sentry duties, we washed and bathed in the Kajaki dam. There were various foreign agencies also operating in the area. One afternoon, members of the ANA retrieved around 100 fish from the dam by throwing a hand grenade into the water. They shallow-fried the fish in lots of oil and served us a welcome feast with some potatoes and fruits.

We occasionally faced indirect fire (IDF) on the mountain from mortars and rockets, but it was mostly inaccurate or fell short. Day and night, we diligently scanned the expansive landscape for any signs of enemy movement. Another persistent nuisance that we had to endure as part of our living conditions was a group of large rats that descended on our rations like a plague. Their gnashing teeth and frantic movements pilfered our food with voracious hunger during the night.

After several weeks, we were relieved in place by the Royal Marine Commandos, who had recently arrived in the country for their upcoming tour. Providing them with a complete handover, my only hope was that their tour would be less ferocious and bloody than it had been for the men and women of 3 PARA Battlegroup, although I didn't hold my breath. At the end of our tour, after enduring over 500 enemy engagements, firing over half a million rounds of small arms, and conducting more than 100 casualty evacuation (CASEVAC) missions, our accomplishments were truly remarkable and showcased our resilience. Sadly, we lost 33 brave soldiers in the process.

15 years later, the withdrawal of Afghanistan was to become a political embarrassment, portraying the best and worst of humanity. It will go down in history as one of the most significant military events of modern times. However, the stories of unparalleled bravery and immense sacrifice deserve to be heard by all and should always be remembered. It is in the sacrifice of individuals that the collective pursuit of peace and freedom finds its most poignant expression, reminding us of the enduring cost of our shared humanity. As the sacrifices of war echo through time, etching their mark on the souls of those who endure them, we should take immense pride in our achievements under what were, at times, incredibly difficult circumstances.

We departed from the war-torn chaos of Kabul a few days later and found ourselves on the tranquil shores of Cyprus for a 24-hour 'decompression' period. The idea seemed almost comical. A military psychologist gave us a brief address. "Should any of you find yourselves struggling with any of the experiences you've had," he explained, his voice carrying a melodic cadence, a tell-tale sign of his refined background, "You should seek support through the appropriate channels." Barely 30 minutes later, we were handed crates of beer, directed to a secluded cove on a private beach, and left to our own devices. What followed can only be described as utter bedlam. Some of the mayhem was captured on film and briefly surfaced on YouTube before being swiftly taken down. Tables and chairs were smashed, and Paratroopers engaged in fights. Some ended up in hospital, all in a disastrously misguided attempt at decompression.

My father had recently been diagnosed with prostate

cancer, and I hadn't seen him in years. Having retired after 22 years of working in Saudi Arabia, he'd bought a villa in Paphos, conveniently just a 40-minute drive from where we were stationed. Given the circumstances, I managed to persuade one of the company sergeant majors to grant me a 12-hour leave of absence. He arranged for an RAF driver to take me to the villa, with plans to pick me up early the next morning. Looking back, I can't help but question the wisdom of my decision. Barely 48 hours prior, I'd been fighting the Taliban. I hadn't had a moment to catch my breath, let alone process the whirlwind of the past several months.

As the car pulls up outside the villa, I take a moment to admire its whitewashed exterior, adorned with terracotta roof tiles. Surrounded by lush greenery, the villa boasts a private garden with olive trees, vibrant flowers, and a vine-covered pergola. It's truly stunning. Stepping out, I approach the door with a sense of trepidation hanging in the air. My scruffy, wild hair and worn-out black 3 PARA Machine Guns platoon t-shirt, torn underneath the arms and across the back, give me a rugged appearance. Paired with flip-flops and US Gulf War One-issued trousers converted into shorts (previous owner a deceased Taliban fighter), I hold a rolled-up cigarette in the corner of my chapped lips. I can only imagine the surprise on my father's face when he opens the door.

Standing there, I feel the weight of a conscientious man's mental torment. His words seem to vanish into thin air, reaching my ears long after they've been spoken, leaving me confused and disoriented. This wasn't the outcome I had expected. Lost in a trance, memories of childhood holidays in Paphos flood my mind, enveloping me in a dreamlike haze.

He looks at me with curiosity. Speaking in a tone barely above a whisper, he says, "Bloody hell, lad. Look at the state of you."
"Alright, Dad. How are you?"
"Come in, I'll get you a beer. Keo ok?"
"Yes, Dad, Keo will do just fine.

10: THE WAR HAS COME HOME

I wake up on the sofa fully dressed, my mouth painfully dry. I roll over onto the floor. Looking down, I see dried blood staining my wrists like a darkened resin. Using the inside of my palm, I rub my eyes in an attempt to bring myself round. I sit up and inhale deeply, the urgency to breathe seizing me. My joints protest with stiffness, and my heart pounds. I'm caught in a momentary panic, rocking back and forth. A sharp intake of air through my nose only intensifies the dizziness. I wretch, but nothing surfaces.

In another room, someone is crying. I stumble to my feet. My left eye won't open. I delicately pick a crust of blood from my eyelashes. It helps a little. My head is throbbing, but through squinted eyes, the room gradually comes into focus, its details emerging from a haze of confusion. My surroundings seem both alien and vaguely familiar, like a dream that refuses to fully dissipate upon waking. The pain in my head intensifies with each passing moment, becoming almost violent. The air feels charged with tension, and my heart is still racing with an anxious rhythm. Trying to piece together the fragments of the night before, I shift my gaze downward once again. The sight brings a wave of nausea. Suddenly, I find myself on the floor, grappling with the disorientation of the moment. "What the fuck happened?" I plead aloud. The words hang in the air, unanswered.

Returning from Afghanistan to England was like stepping into a world that no longer recognised me. Home no longer held the familiarity I desperately craved. It stretched out before me like an unfamiliar landscape, leaving me lost in a boundless sea of uncertainty, unsure of where to find solid ground. Adjusting to this new reality felt like trying to grasp smoke—intangible and elusive. Instead of finding refuge in the recognisable, my days became a battleground, where the only respite came in the form of alcohol's numbing embrace.

Night after night, as exhaustion finally claimed me, I found myself thrust into a relentless onslaught of memories. No sooner would I close my eyes than I'd be consumed by vivid recollections, drowning in waves of guilt, neuroticism, and fear. None of it made sense. Sleep became my greatest adversary. I would jolt awake during the night, gasping for air, my heartbeat drumming loudly against the silence. In those fleeting moments of wakefulness, I was a soldier once more, my body poised for battle against an invisible enemy. With trembling hands, I would fumble in the darkness, searching desperately for a rifle and my helmet. But all I found was the hollow emptiness of my room and the echoes of a war I'd fought thousands of miles away, taunting me from the shadows.

As I drag myself into the next room, feeling like a wounded animal emerging from thorny undergrowth, fragments of memories emerge from the gloom. We invited my brother and sister-in-law over to the house for a meal and a few drinks. That much I remember. The conversations were nothing more than background noise, a mumbling chatter akin to what you might hear in a shopping centre or a classroom.

Terrifying intrusive thoughts of Afghanistan would consume my mind. Sometimes, I would make a fist and physically beat my head in a hopeless effort to rid myself of them.

I'm beginning to remember what happened now: we were drinking. My sister-in-law, Claire, with her vibrant red hair and freckles, possessed a dark sense of humour and sharp wit that could catch people off guard, but

Beyond the Drop Zone

I liked her. After one too many glasses of wine, she'd started play-fighting with me. Like a spar in boxing, we'd playfully shadowboxed in the kitchen. I'd hunched over, fists pressed against my head, allowing her to land blows on me, one after another. I'd strangely enjoyed the pain. It was the first thing I'd felt in weeks—the sensation of bone against bone had stirred emotions within me that I hadn't known existed.

Suddenly, I'd been overcome with a feeling of self-hatred and rage, seemingly out of nowhere, my head pounding as if it were a train on the tracks. Physically trembling and hyperventilating, I'd started punching myself in the face, both fists clenched, each blow harder than the last. Crying out and afraid, I'd blackened both of my eyes and bloodied my nose, overwhelmed by uncontrollable sadness. My brother-in-law, Ryan, had leapt across the kitchen and thrown both of his arms around me in a desperate attempt to stop me from attacking myself. We'd crashed onto the side of the kitchen worktop, crying, bruised, and bloodied.

In the midst of the mayhem, I'd noticed the large, black handle of a kitchen knife in my periphery. With trembling hands, I'd reached out and grabbed the knife from the wooden knife block and slashed at my wrists. Blood had immediately began pouring out, a tangible release for my anger and indescribable sadness. It had streamed down my palm and along my fingers, eventually dripping off my fingertips like a tap. Was this truly what I wanted? How had it come to this?

As the story of the night reveals itself to me, I crouch down on the kitchen floor and wrap my arms around my head, like an animal protecting itself against a predator. Again, I wonder… How had it come to this?

It was Christmas 2006, and it was cold outside. The sky was enveloped in a deep, velvety black, and the air was sharp with the bite of frost. At that time, I'd only been married for a few years. I'd met Sarah in Colchester. She was a local girl, and we'd perhaps rushed into marriage a little hastily, tying the knot soon after my return from Iraq. We were both only 18. Sarah was pregnant with our son, Owen, throughout my deployment to Afghanistan. He arrived only weeks after I got home, leaving me grappling with the whirlwind of fatherhood whilst also desperately trying to make sense of what I'd experienced during the past several months.

Sarah moved out of the house that night, taking baby Owen with her. Days later, she told me she thought she was going to die that night. I responded with one of the most selfish, merciless remarks possible: "Welcome to my world." I felt utterly emotionless—numb, robot-like, and unnaturally calm. I also felt profoundly alienated from those who hadn't experienced Afghanistan, who hadn't been on that rooftop. The phrase 'losing one's mind' suggests a gradual decline. When there is no tangible connection to our surroundings, existence unfolds as a haunting chorus reverberating through vacant chambers—an eerie symphony of self-expression.

Outside, a gust of wind sends a whirlwind of leaves soaring into the December sky. The leaves are starting to glimmer silver, introducing a hint of coolness in the air. As I peer out the back door, I sense something isn't right. Despite being physically present, I feel incredibly alone and detached from reality. This creeping sensory numbness and the deterioration of my decision-making abilities are not the only issues associated with my feelings. I question whether I have a future on this earth at all.

What exactly is trauma? It's an internal injury, the aftermath of a difficult event. It feels like a heavy weight pressing down on the chest, making every breath a struggle. It's not merely about external occurrences; rather, it's about the internal aftermath. While the event itself may pass, the lasting injury remains, and even the slightest stimuli can reopen the wound, causing an endless cycle of pain. The effects of trauma are profound—it's a wound that penetrates your very psyche. It alters how you cope, how you interact, and how you perceive the world around you. Its influence extends to your closest relationships and leaves a lasting imprint on every aspect of your life.

Alcohol appeared to offer temporary respite. With each sip, a numbing sensation would wash over me, softening the edges of both reality's demands and the existential horrors lurking in my mind. As the sun dipped below the horizon, casting long shadows across the living room of my garrison home, the bottle became my evening companion. I found myself compulsively drinking to excess, seeking an antidote, however fleeting, to the relentless intrusion of my own thoughts. As the first waves of intoxication washed over me, I welcomed the numbness, the brief hush that alcohol offered, like a long-lost friend.

It was a futile attempt at escape, though; I could never hope to truly silence the haunting whispers constantly circling the dark corridors of my mind. The demons of my past taunted me with memories I wished desperately to erase. With each crisp, satisfying pop of a ring-pull, followed by the faint hiss of escaping gas from a fresh can of lager, I found myself grappling with the paradox of seeking escape while feeling trapped within the confines of my own mind.

On top of emerging alcohol dependency, the destructiveness of sleep deprivation also began pervading every aspect of my life. In Afghanistan, whether on that rooftop or out on patrol, crippling fear had made me hyper-alert, intensifying colours and sounds. Back home, however, trauma drained colours of their vibrancy. The world now bore the pallid, grainy semblance of a weathered newspaper photograph. I became too scared to fall asleep because of the horrendous nightmares that awaited me. Yet staying awake meant being bombarded by equally terrifying thoughts. Despite Sarah's efforts, my only escape seemed to be drowning myself in alcohol. I would sit alone, littering the table with a growing pile of crumpled Kronenbourg 1664 cans, enveloped by emptiness and the lingering scent of stale beer and cigarettes. Eventually, with trembling hands, I would reach for the whiskey bottle, its amber contents seeming to offer a deeper escape from the suffocating weight of reality.

I developed a warped coping strategy, obsessively accumulating and watching execution videos I found on the internet—people suffering and dying in all manner of horrendous ways. I would sit and focus on every detail, hoping to feel something, but nothing came. And then came more alcohol. No matter how hard I tried, I found myself trapped in an endless loop, replaying those moments in the theatre of my mind. Overthinking had always been my relentless companion, but now it became a curse that clung to my thoughts like a shadow. Night after night, I reached for the cans and then the bottle. One drink would turn into several, and before I knew it, I was drowning my sorrows yet again. It was my desperate attempt to find solace in the oblivion of unconsciousness.

By this point, my marriage had unravelled and spiralled drastically into decline. It was no surprise, really. I felt as though I were wandering in a perpetual dream, disconnected from the world I once knew, lost in a maze of my own thoughts, and I didn't know how to ask for help. Not a day went by when I didn't think of Afghanistan in some way. More often than not, it was in the stillness of the night, as my subconscious roamed freely, that haunting memories resurfaced. Occasionally, the trigger was as innocuous as a scent or an unexpected sound, whether it be the creaking of a door, the shattering of a plate, or, in the most distressing instances, a firework. I would literally tear clumps of hair from my head and gnaw at my fingernails incessantly until I drew blood. As the blood dried, it would cling stubbornly to the edges of my fingers, its rusty hue contrasting starkly against my pale skin. It would take me right back to carrying Paddy off that mud compound roof after he'd been shot through his neck.

The most distressing symptom of trauma is reliving an event, whether you want to or not. This re-experiencing can take the form of recurrent nightmares or daytime flashbacks. In either case, you're faced with vivid, repetitive pictures of the trauma. Sometimes, the pictures are so real that you behave as though the event is happening all over again. Most of the time, it's just for a few seconds, adding fuel to the erroneous belief that you are 'going mad'. The event is usually in picture form, but sounds and smells can act as triggers to start the picture sequence.

For me, it became a vicious circle. I would become so anxious that I would feel like I was drowning. An overwhelming rush of emotions would consume my whole body, and in that instant, I was back in Afghanistan. Not just thinking about Afghanistan. Actually believing I was there.

Family members and friends don't usually know how to react to such terrifying behaviour, and why should they? This makes the whole experience even worse. You begin trying to avoid any situations that could trigger flashbacks, which only causes more panic, and then you begin to lose contact with others, making yourself even more isolated.

It was most challenging when these kinds of anxious surges occurred in public places, like bustling restaurants or bars. My inability to stifle my involuntary hyper-response to situations was deeply embarrassing. Curious gazes would fixate on me, casting me as an oddity. Perhaps the most exasperating aspect was the lack of control—I would have involuntary flinches that left me feeling powerless in the face of judgmental stares.

Then I just began feeling so desperately sad all the time. I would find myself in tears over seemingly trivial matters like TV shows. Emotions would unexplainably surge within me, and I would well up. I would bite the inside of my cheek to stop myself from crying, and I made a concerted effort to conceal it from those around me. Dr Gravewell later explained to me that this was caused by a neurological split—a heightened sensitivity to stimuli that can occur after traumatic events. It's a parallel similar to when psychopaths struggle to connect with emotions like empathy and compassion. I felt as though the part of my brain that regulated feelings and emotions was broken.

The demons persisted, but eventually, a glimmer of self-awareness whispered that, perhaps, amidst the shadows, there existed a path toward the light. I had contemplated taking my own life on so many occasions, but finally, Sarah was able to get me referred to see a clinical psychologist through a military medical officer.

Dr Alexander Gravewell was an enigmatic psychologist who exuded an aura of intellectual intrigue, captivating anyone who spoke with him. He had a meticulously groomed dark beard and penetrating eyes below heavy, furrowed eyebrows that arched like thunderclouds heavy with the promise of revelation. Draped in tailored suits, he radiated quiet authority, embodying a psychologist with a profound understanding of the human psyche. I owe him my life.

What I struggled to understand was why this had affected me so ruthlessly and others not at all. Dr Gravewell had two theories. One is that these shared experiences affected more people than I was ever aware of, or that symptoms presented themselves much later in life. The other, which I believe, used the ironic simile of a pint glass. The trauma experienced in one's life is stored inside this pint glass—childhood trauma, predisposition to mental health problems, family breakups, and any other innate and external factors. Eventually, that glass overflows, leading to a neurological split. Something gives way, and that is the point where a person may experience a breakdown, psychosis, or other manifestation of the mind's attempt to cope with these issues.

Ultimately, I was diagnosed with Complex Post-Traumatic Stress Disorder (PTSD). Little did I know that these few words would reshape the landscape of my life. The struggle was not confined to external battles; it was internal warfare, a daily confrontation with memories that had become haunting spectres. Managing the condition became my only focus for stability, a goal that often felt frustratingly just beyond reach. Therapy sessions continued for several months, and these included medications, Cognitive Behavioural Therapy (CBT), and the journaling that eventually led me to write this book. Although there were moments of resilience, the journey was not straightforward; it was a maze of progress and setbacks, of small victories and humbling defeats. Relationships became a delicate dance between disclosure and concealment. The fear of judgement hung heavy, and the simplest of tasks became monumental challenges as the disorder remained stubbornly intertwined with the fabric of my daily life.

PTSD changed my life indefinitely. The person I was before had essentially died, and a new 'me' emerged: one tempered by adversity and marked by scars that were unseen but deeply felt. The most mundane tasks became infused with emotional complexity, and things that I'd always taken to be ordinary became extraordinary now that I truly appreciated how fragile life was. I found solace in the smallest of rituals—the steady cadence of deep breaths, the reassurance of a support system, and the deliberate steps toward self-acceptance. Yet, my reliance on alcohol as an escape brought its own physical health issues to mental dependency.

Although I've never stopped drinking completely, I did manage to change my relationship with alcohol, becoming less dependent on it to 'cope' when life became overwhelming. The past would attempt to pull me back, like heavy chains refusing to let me move forward. During long periods working in the Middle East, I practised complete abstinence, which helped me develop different coping mechanisms.

It's worth mentioning that none of this was without drastic failures, even to this day. When my mind wanders or I am triggered, becoming desperately sad or reflective, the urge to binge claws at me like a relentless beast, tempting me to drink myself into an oblivion where nothing else matters. It promises peace and seductive escape if I just surrender to a destructive predisposition to alcoholism. But I resist, most of the time, because that's not what they would want. By 'they', I mean the poor young souls who never came home or who succumbed to their demons and took their own lives. When the craving to blot everything out with alcohol is strong, I think of them. I have been given the invaluable gift of time, and I intend to make the most of it. True resolution comes only by addressing the root causes of the desire to escape and finding healthier, more sustainable coping mechanisms.

Living with PTSD isn't about quick fixes but about committing to healing. The extreme reactions—the flashbacks and self-harming—can dissipate over time, but it requires patience, self-compassion, and an unwavering belief that, despite the storms within, there is a possibility of calm. Being diagnosed was a pivotal moment in my life, but that doesn't mean that it dictates the entire narrative. Instead, it's a testament to the power of resilience, a story of survival, and a reminder that even in the darkest times of your life, light can still emerge. With time, therapy, and support, healing is attainable. Though the journey may be arduous, remember that you are not defined by your trauma, and there is blue sky beyond even the blackest of storms.

Life can be wonderful and tragic and cruel all at the same time, but the path to healing is to remember it without reliving it.

Beyond the Drop Zone

A vacant, unfocused gaze, often referred to as a 'thousand-yard stare', after enduring a Taliban ambush and hours of intense fighting.

Back at Camp Bastion after 49 days of fighting in the Sangin District.

Captured upon impact: the aftermath of a JDAM bomb hitting its target.

Iraqi Security Forces advance on a village in Western Mosul following the launch of an offensive to retake it from ISIS. Note the damage to the windscreen from bullets.

The 'Golden Division', along with Peshmerga fighters, led Iraq to victory in the siege of Mosul against ISIS. One is seen here wearing their infamous skull mask.

Kurdish Peshmerga forces capture a network of tunnels in a village that were being used by ISIS snipers. These tunnels were booby-trapped with IEDs.

Beyond the Drop Zone

Close protection in Iraq: Inside one of our B6 armoured Toyota Land Cruisers used for convoys. Note the chest-mounted pistol and AK-47 assault rifle stored in the footwell.

Hostile environment training in Tunisia shortly after an ISIS gunman opened fire indiscriminately at tourists on the beach at a popular resort, killing 38 people.

Beyond the Drop Zone

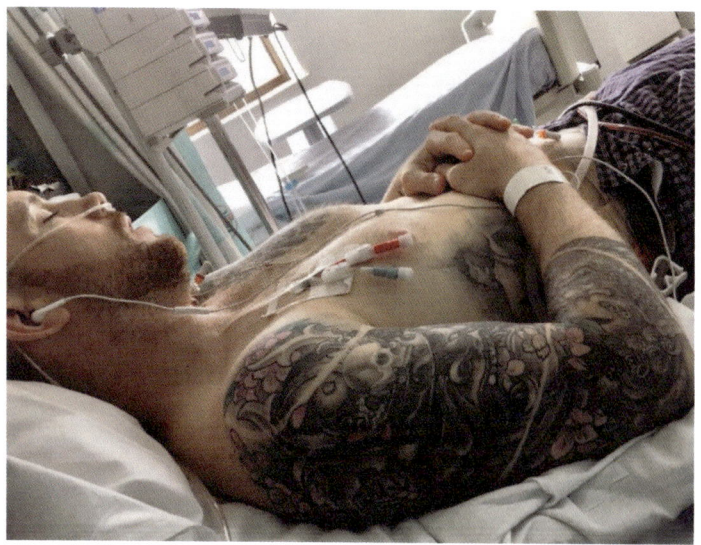

Battling end stage renal failure, relying on the life-saving support of Hemodialysis while lying in a hospital bed.

Practising Muay Thai in a basic gym in southern Thailand. I lived in Thailand for several years while working in the close protection industry, rotating between assignments in the Middle East.

Beyond the Drop Zone

A snapshot of my sister and me at my fire service pass-out parade.

In 2019, on the day of our wedding, my wife Louise and my son Owen captured in a heartfelt moment that will forever be cherished.

11: A NEW MISSION

"Danny," I call, my voice concealing a hint of unease, "take your vehicle and push ahead to the vantage point on that high ground." The landscape stretching out before us is vast and unwelcoming. I scan it for any signs of danger. "Let me know immediately if you spot anything out of the ordinary, mate."

In military jargon, 'eyes on' is the phrase that signifies the critical act of identifying a potential threat. We scouted for Toyota pickup trucks adorned with ominous black flags in the distance. Danny, with his deep-set, earthy eyes, stood as an embodiment of strength and reliability. His broad Sunderland 'Mackem' accent, worn like a badge of honour, resonated with authenticity. His body was a canvas of tattoos that told the stories of his life, and he exuded an air of unwavering determination. He was as fit as they come and not only a close protection colleague but also a friend I'd weathered countless missions with. On this day in 2011, as we ventured further into the unknown, I knew without a doubt that I could trust him implicitly.

I'd been tasked with exploring an overland route for our American clients, leading them safely out of Iraq and into the sanctuary of Kuwait. Baghdad International Airport had shuttered its doors in response to a relentless barrage of IDF rocket and mortar attacks that had targeted it in recent days. In addition to this threat, there had been various intelligence reports suggesting that ISIL cells were operating in the area. ISIL, or the Islamic State of Iraq and the Levant, was a jihadist group affiliated with al-Qaeda. They'd become notorious during the insurgency that followed the coalition's invasion of Iraq in 2003. In April 2013, amid a bitter feud, ISIL split from al-Qaeda and rebranded itself as the Islamic State of Iraq and Syria (ISIS). Distinguished by its unparalleled brutality, ISIS soon eclipsed even the notorious Syrian jihadist group Jabhat al-Nusra in terms of sheer ruthlessness. Within months, its forces had ruthlessly carved out a dominion extending across the expanse of eastern Syria and western Iraq.

During this period, I was working in the sun-scorched south of Iraq, providing close protection to employees of a large oil and gas organisation. This generally meant spending several months 'in-country' at a time. I facilitated convoys to various government offices, spanning the region that stretched south from the Baghdad Belts of Iraq to Kuwait, also referred to as Lower Mesopotamia. Mesopotamia, translated as the 'Land between the Rivers', alludes to the ancient Euphrates and Tigris rivers.

The barren-brown Arabian desert was excruciatingly hot. It had an intense, almost spiteful wrath that bore down on us constantly. The land was flat and arid, and only the occasional brittle bush broke the emptiness of the plains. The air was cloying and sticky, and a constant, virulent smell of concrete and dust hung upon it, becoming chained inside my nostrils. It quickly became the only ever-present companion besides misery.

We generally wore non-script clothing—cargo pants, ballistic plate carrier, and Kevlar helmet—similar to those worn by UK Special Forces at the time. The border crossing took roughly two hours by convoy, navigating primarily along undulating dirt-track roads. My team travelled in four armoured Toyota Land Cruisers, each operated by local nationals. These Iraqi drivers, or LNs as they were commonly known, were mostly recruited from nearby villages and towns. Some of them had previously worked for the coalition forces during the war, which explained their noticeable American accents. Danny served as my second-in-command (2IC), while I held the position of team leader.

Before each mission, I led an exhaustive team briefing, outlining the primary and secondary routes and preparing for a range of contingencies, including potential 'what if' scenarios. These discussions encompassed situations such as encountering checkpoints, handling a medical emergency during the mission, responding to a vehicle in the convoy being hit by an IED, and dealing with possible communication disruptions.

Danny's face is a mask of shock as he urgently gestures for me to cast my gaze across the endless expanse of desolation. The sun is beating down relentlessly, casting harsh shadows over the rugged terrain. I follow his desperate gesture, squinting against the blinding light, and there, amidst the unforgiving landscape, my heart is a relentless drumbeat, its pace reflecting the fear pulsing through my veins. A worn-out, stained white pick-up truck has materialised on the horizon, its battered frame a stark contrast against the barren backdrop. The sight of it alone is enough to put us on edge, but as it moves closer, we discern the dreaded black-and-white flag of ISIS flapping above it in the searing breeze. Despite the oppressive heat, we are instantly chilled to the core.

In that heart-pounding moment, a surge of adrenaline erupts within me, coursing through my thoughts like wildfire. Yet, this strange euphoria is swiftly overshadowed by trepidation and a profound sense of amazed horror, as the gravity of the unfolding situation comes crashing down upon me. The pick-up, its malevolent monochrome banner proclaiming, "There is no God but Allah", maintains a discreet distance from our convoy, like a predator stalking its prey. It becomes apparent that, for the moment at least, we're not their intended target, perhaps because we're now nearly at the Kuwaiti border. However, the stark reality of the situation tempers any sense of relief. Although the truck is distant, we can still identify the ominous silhouettes of long-barrelled weapons and automatic rifles protruding from its open windows. Danger is very much on our tail.

This was my first encounter with ISIS. It was a chilling experience that would leave an indelible mark on my memory, and it wasn't to be my last.

It was a volatile time across the entire Middle East. The Iraq War finally ended with the withdrawal of US forces in December 2011 (British troops had left six months beforehand). One year earlier, however, almost to the day, a young Tunisian street vendor named Mohamed Bouazizi had set himself on fire after being harassed by police, publicly humiliated by local authorities, and having his wares confiscated. When he died from his injuries, the protests became so fierce and widespread that the Tunisian president fled the country. This episode led to what became known as the 'Arab Spring', with protests and anti-government demonstrations in Libya, Egypt, Bahrain, Yemen and Syria amongst other places.

This widespread unrest led to a noticeable surge in the demand for 'protective services', particularly in environments marked by hostility and formidable challenges. Such services encompassed a wide spectrum of responsibilities, including providing close protection to commercial clients and undertaking outsourced military missions. They could also involve the crucial role of training national military forces, journalists, and non-governmental organisations (NGOs), something I would later specialise in.

At that time, the concept of security advisors was relatively nascent. They were professional operators who typically worked closely with governments that had strong alliances with their home countries or adhered to international legal frameworks. Notably, many of these security advisors possessed backgrounds rooted in military experience, lending them the necessary expertise and skills to navigate the complex and hazardous environments they encountered. This period marked a pivotal moment in the evolution of protective services, as they became increasingly essential in a world rife with security challenges. I'd left the Paras in February 2009, and the 'circuit', as it was commonly known, felt like a natural progression for someone with my background. Close protection, sometimes known as personal security or bodyguarding, entails the provision of security and safeguarding services to individuals or groups vulnerable to potential harm or targeting for various motives. The foremost objective is to ensure the safety and welfare of those under protection.

Following the Iraq War, the circumstances were favourable for security firms to seize numerous contracts related to oil extraction. I used what resettlement funds I had accrued during my service with the Paras and enrolled in a three-month close protection course in Hereford. The course was highly esteemed, being led by two of the most seasoned and highly regarded figures in the field. It marked the beginning of my career in close protection, starting with employment with the Crown Service in Central London. It is a chapter I am unable and unwilling to divulge due to specific legislation, namely The Official Secrets Act. What I can say, however, is that my responsibilities included delivering protective services for government dignitaries and foreign agencies visiting the United Kingdom, as well as escorting covert human intelligence sources (CHIS). Close protection services, as I quickly learned, can vary widely depending on the specific needs and circumstances of the individuals or groups being protected. Such services are often sought by high-profile individuals, celebrities, dignitaries, and individuals at risk due to their professions or personal circumstances.

Several years later, I transitioned to a new phase of my career, one that revolved around safeguarding high-profile personalities and catering to the needs of the super-rich. This journey led me back to London, where I dedicated another year to this demanding profession. While the role kept me tirelessly occupied, with long hours spent within the confines of five-star hotels, upscale dining establishments, and frequent journeys to luxurious destinations like the south of France and other parts of Europe, it was not without its challenges. Although it might have seemed relatively low-risk on the surface, it was a job that proved instrumental in honing essential interpersonal skills unique to the world of close protection. Every task brought its own set of complexities and dangers, from navigating through public disorder events to ensuring the safety of clients in unfamiliar and potentially hostile environments, including some undercover deployments.

However, despite the demanding nature of the work, an opportunity presented itself for me to deploy back to the Middle East, and I took it. My decision was driven not only by the prospect of substantial opportunities and financial rewards but also by a desire to immerse myself once again in the fast-moving and evolving landscape of hostile environments—it was a new set of challenges to overcome.

Securing a position with one of the most highly respected companies of the time was a significant milestone in my career journey. The close protection industry had quickly become saturated, so even getting your foot in the door came with its own challenges. I had to successfully complete the company's rigorous internal selection course, with no guarantee of employment at the end. HEAT (Hostile Environment Awareness Training) is a specialised form of stress exposure training meticulously crafted to empower individuals with the necessary skills for navigating the diverse risk environments they may encounter. The training blends theoretical learning with hands-on practical experience and encompasses comprehensive pre-hospital care tailored for those operating in challenging and remote settings. Against the backdrop of a world grappling with unprecedented challenges, including geopolitical risks, pandemics, regional conflicts, terrorism, and escalating organised and opportunistic crime, the selection process had to be robust.

During one scenario, I found myself stepping into a meticulously designed simulation building that replicated the infamous 'Killing House' utilised by the United Kingdom

Special Forces (UKSF) for honing counter-terrorism and close-quarters battle (CQB) skills. This immersive setting boasted movable partitions, smoke machines, pyrotechnics for illumination and signalling, and a repertoire of battle noises and effects. To heighten the realism, the facility also incorporated casualty simulation (CASSIM), which was capable of replicating a wide range of traumatic injuries. From gunshot wounds and fragmentation impacts to various other trauma effects tailored to specific scenarios—burns, chemical exposure, acid contact—CASSIM aimed to deliver an authentic and intense training experience.

"Alright, listen in!" declares one of the directing staff (DS) as he sets the stage to brief my team. "Navigate through the building and tend to any casualties you come across." The atmosphere is heavy with anticipation, foreshadowing an upcoming whirlwind of rapid movement, disorder, and noise. Without missing a beat, he presses on. "Inspect the contents of your grab bags." A grab bag in this instance means a portable repository of essentials, a lifeline to snatch in the event of a sudden evacuation when there's no time for second thoughts. "The scenario will test your knowledge and the practical application of the course in a high-pressure environment." I swiftly inspect each medical item within the grab bag—tourniquets poised at the top and airway management tools standing ready for the orchestrated chaos that awaits.

In teams of two, we enter the building, methodically clearing each room and assessing casualties as they are presented to us. The first casualty, a priority one, has sustained a gunshot wound to his upper left thigh, resulting in a catastrophic haemorrhage from a ruptured femoral artery. Quickly, we apply a tourniquet and mark the time of application before dragging him to safety, all while continuing our building clearance.

The next casualty we encounter is unconscious and not breathing. Throughout the exercise, the simulation is intensified by battlefield noises and pyrotechnics, immersing us in a realistic training environment. As we assess the casualty, it becomes clear that she requires a tracheostomy due to a blast wound and compromised airway. This surgical procedure involves creating an opening in the neck to access the trachea, allowing for direct airway access when breathing through the mouth or nose is impaired. The DS pause the drill and lead us to another compartment where we are presented with the anatomy of a pig's neck, throat, and trachea attached to a short length of timber. Next to it lies an array of surgical tools that will allow us to perform the tracheostomy under time and pressure constraints.

I relished every part of the training. The instructors were the best in their field, and the rest of the candidates on the course mostly came from UKSF, the Paras, or the Royal Marines—all highly-trained and experienced professional operators. The training culminated in a two-day close protection and surveillance exercise for which I was designated the position of team leader.

I soon found myself deployed back to Iraq on an oil and gas assignment, assuming the dual role of 'shooter' and medic. My primary responsibility was to ensure the safety and security of individuals or assets being transported. This involved assessing threats through reconnaissance and analysing intelligence. Additionally, I maintained clear communication channels between the convoy and the operations room. In the event of an emergency, such as an attack or accident, I was responsible for providing medical assistance, evacuation support, or, if necessary, engaging the threat. We also trained all locally employed Iraqi nationals in trauma care, defensive driving tactics, and convoy manoeuvres. This chapter marked the beginning of my adventure into a world fraught with unique experiences and opportunities.

The Middle East has always held a profound fascination for me, and that allure remains undiminished. Perhaps it stems from my childhood years spent in Saudi Arabia, when I was exposed to a culture vastly different from anything I had previously encountered. Modern-day Iraq, however, couldn't be more different. It bears the deep scars of years of war and conflict. Over the past two decades, the nation has grappled with the devastation of the Iraq War and its aftermath, including the rise of various insurgents and the emergence of ISIS. Kidnappings and roadside bombs were significant security concerns when I was deployed back out there in 2010, necessitating an exhaustive level of planning for travel and operations within the country. Additionally, there was the presence of various armed groups, both Sunni and Shia, to contend with. It all contributed to the complexity of its already fragile security landscape.

12: THE HORNET'S NEST

In 2015, after several years of close protection work, I was given the opportunity to work in freelance high-risk consulting. This involved providing training and support to organisations operating in hostile and challenging environments across the world. Some of our clients included multinational corporations, charities, NGOs, media networks, government departments, and sectors of the construction and aviation industries. The work involved delivering a comprehensive range of specialist training programs to prepare these clients for what they might encounter. Over a period of five years, I operated in most of the world's most challenging environments, from the plains of Africa to fragile states in the Middle East, North Africa, and Asia.

I had just finished teaching a HEAT course in Hereford for an NGO client travelling to South Sudan to cover the civil unrest unfolding there. As the course drew to a close, I requested to visit headquarters. I was sitting in the reception area when the door swung open, revealing a figure shrouded in an aura of mystery. He was a battle-hardened veteran of the legendary UKSF, a man whose reputation was known throughout the secretive corridors of our industry.

This man, who can't be named, ushered me to a dimly lit briefing room, where a mosaic of intelligence reports lay before me, each fragment meticulously detailing the complex political landscape of the foreign land I was about to enter. With a voice as rugged as his past exploits, he leaned across the cluttered desk and asked, "Can you deploy to Kurdistan on Sunday?"

"No problem," I replied as casually as I could. "What's the task?"

The room seemed to hold its breath. With a measured nod, he finally divulged, "You will act as a security advisor for a media team of American clients."

I leaned forward, my anticipation growing. "Okay," I replied, eager to hear more of the details.

"What is your current knowledge of the region like?" His gaze bore into mine, assessing my readiness for the challenge.

I leaned back in my chair, memories of dusty landscapes flooding back. "I've operated in and around the area for several years," I began, my mind retracing its steps through the years and the various deployments. "I was last there in April, assisting a media team to navigate their way out of Syria."

He regarded me for a moment, and then, as if to test the depth of my familiarity, he gestured to a blank piece of paper on the desk. "Draw a map of the area from memory." I reached for a pen and began to sketch the contours of the region. I included major cities, borders, and rivers that took shape on the paper, a testament to the years of experience I'd spent navigating the region's geography. Once I'd completed my makeshift map, he examined it with a scrutinising eye, his silence revealing nothing. After a minute or so, he finally spoke: "See Katie for an intelligence update." With a barely perceptible lift of his index finger, he directed my attention to the far corner of the office and to the next chapter of my life.

I deployed with a crew of three American journalists to cover the Mosul offensive by the Peshmerga Kurdish Forces and Iraqi Special Forces, known in Iraq as the 'Golden Division', in October 2016. Just over two years previously, the city of Mosul, Iraq's second-largest city, housing approximately two million residents, had succumbed to the still-strong ISIS. Under the leadership of Abu Abdulrahman al-Bilawi, the insurgent group had managed to vanquish the Iraqi army from the city.

By this time, ISIS had a global reputation for barbarity. They had destroyed the boundaries of contemporary nation-states and proclaimed themselves restorers of a lost Islamic empire, arguably becoming more extreme than their former allies, al-Qaeda. ISIS aimed to re-establish their supposedly lost empire through their extreme interpretation of Sharia law. In just a few years, they had managed to capture significant territory in Iraq and Syria and become infamous for their brutal tactics, including public executions, hostage beheadings, and mass killings. They had also enslaved and brutalised minority groups, particularly the Yazidis and Christians—they executed 19 Yazidi women by burning them alive in iron cages because they refused to become sex slaves. I was later to witness the aftermath of their cruelty first-hand.

The purpose of my deployment was to provide health, safety, and security advice, plus medical assistance if required, to the news team being deployed to Kurdistan. Additionally, I would relay relevant intelligence to analysts regarding the ongoing situation and developments on the ground.

I rendezvous with our fixer, Rahim, who will prove invaluable to the success of the mission, and we discuss Mosul's uncertain security climate. Huddled in a dimly lit boardroom of the Divan Hotel in Erbil, the stark reality of the situation on the ground hangs heavy in the air. Rahim's tall, lean figure reveals a man worn by experiences too heavy for his years. His eyes are shadowed by thick-set eyebrows, and he speaks with an unexpected but oddly familiar American twang to his accent. He'd been embedded with the Italian Army at Mosul Dam. He begins telling me about how their camp had been mercilessly targeted by placed explosive devices, three of which had detonated the previous night. The ever-present threat looms large, exacerbated by the constant presence of coalition forces in the vicinity.

At 4 pm, we depart the relative sanctuary of the hotel and make our way to the airport to collect the media crew. All routes to and from the city are demarcated by an array of checkpoints, each vigilantly manned by Iraqi secret police in plain clothing. There are four to six officers at each checkpoint. Their vehicles are ominous black pickups armed with mounted medium machine guns, pistols, and an assortment of AK-47 variants.

An estimated 4,000 to 5,000 ISIS militants are believed to be active in Mosul. After we collect the media crew, the editor, John, receives a phone call from Atlanta, bringing a glimmer of hope amid the tension. The Head of Security for Masood Barzani, leader of the Kurdistan Democratic Party, has granted us permission for a shot with the Peshmerga on the frontline. The Peshmerga, whose name translates as 'those who face death', are Kurdish fighters in northern Iraq. They're currently involved in heavy fighting with ISIS in Kalak, near the outskirts of Mosul.

Upon our return to Erbil, we regroup at the Divan Hotel, where I introduce the media team to Rahim and our local driver companions. The contrast between the gleaming marble floors of this luxurious establishment and the gritty backdrop of Mosul is, to say the least, a culture shock.

We gather over cups of chai tea, and the focus shifts to the evening's mission. As we delve into the details of the planning, I subtly observe our team members, scrutinising their movements and body language. It's my silent attempt at gauging their comfort with risk, their aspirations for this journey, and any potential limitations. Bill, the lead anchorman, is a towering figure in the world of war reporting. He stands tall and assertive, his once-ebony hair now gracefully sporting streaks of grey and silver. He exudes an unmistakable charismatic charm. "Hey Andy, what's the latest on the ground?" he asks.

"The Peshmerga and ISIS are still locked in ongoing skirmishes," I reply. "And the condition of the roads is giving us legitimate cause for worry. Yesterday, another team rolled a vehicle, resulting in two severe injuries, including a ruptured spleen. They had to be rushed to a US field hospital."

"Think we can make it to Kalak this evening?" he asks, his gaze steady.

"It's entirely plausible," I say. "Our greatest challenge will be navigating the checkpoints. Fortunately, Rahim's cousin is an officer in the Iraqi

Army. He's confident that he can help us pass through the checkpoints."

The Iraqi security forces would indeed prove to be exceptionally welcoming and cooperative. They were eager to have us document the pivotal battle of Mosul, as they were determined to reclaim the city and showcase their courageous triumph to a global audience.

It took me 40 minutes to carry out a comprehensive check of all the essential equipment aboard our B6 Armoured Land Cruisers—trauma bags, ballistic body armour, and communications. We discussed diverse scenarios and developed contingency plans. I was satisfied with how the teams responded, and I came up with a preliminary strategy for the approaching days, acknowledging the necessity of adaptability in response to the ever-evolving dynamics on the ground.

We arrived in Kalak the same evening, and the scene was one of frenetic activity. Peshmerga forces flooded the Mosul Road, their tanks and lorries brimming with determined fighters and a cache of impressive weaponry. Masses of local residents and tribal leaders lined the road, their cheers echoing in a deafening chorus and their smartphones capturing the momentous occasion.

Iraqi security forces appeared to be well-equipped with a variety of weapons, armoured vehicles, anti-tank weapons, tanks, artillery, and Mine-Resistant Ambush Protected (MRAP) vehicles. The latter were designed to increase survivability for the crews inside against improvised explosive devices, mines, and ambushes. As the columns of vehicles passed us, they proudly waved the tricolour flag of the Kurdish people—red, white, and green, with the golden sun emblem at the centre, an important symbol of Kurdish identity. I made eye contact with one of the soldiers perched on top of a vehicle. He defiantly raised one arm above his head and gestured a peace sign towards me. It was clear to me that they were ready to take the fight to ISIS and reclaim Mosul at all costs.

Beyond the Drop Zone

We met with a Peshmerga field commander, Fahad, and the gravity of the situation was unmistakable. Alongside other journalists, we were informed that the impending offensive was scheduled to commence late in the morning of 17th October. The words resonated with an air of history in the making. A further announcement by Haider al-Abadi stated that Mosul was teetering on the brink of liberation. ISIS had controlled the city and much of northern and western Iraq for over two years. It was unknown how long the actual offensive could take. One of the main concerns was the displacement of up to 1.5 million civilians fleeing the city. There had been attempts to facilitate migrant corridors to Internal Displaced Person (IDP) camps like Dibaga, which we had visited, to the southeast of the city.

The following morning, an estimated 30,000 Iraqi troops, including the Golden Brigade, Kurdish Peshmerga fighters, Sunni Arab tribesmen, and Shia militiamen, assisted by US-led coalition warplanes, started the offensive. It was a peculiar sight to see village elders dressed in traditional clothing carrying hunting rifles, ready to fight with all they had.

The Peshmerga secured a number of villages near Khazir to the east, and we pushed forward to the outskirts of Bartella, where ISIS had attempted to erect temporary barriers along the highway in an effort to prevent vehicles from passing. The barriers were constructed from tyres, and some had been set on fire to reduce visibility and impede air operations. Whilst there, we examined some of the underground tunnel systems built by ISIS. Some of the entrances were booby-trapped with IEDs and marked with painted stones and metal posts driven into the ground. As I cautiously crept through the abandoned enemy encampment, signs of recent occupancy became evident. Among the rubble and debris, I stumbled upon makeshift sleeping quarters, where simple bedding lay strewn about in disarray. It was a cramped space where nearby, scattered metal cooking pots caught my eye, littered around a *dallah* (a traditional Arabic coffee pot) sat atop an improvised stove, its surface still warm from the heat of the flames. Their presence lingered in the air, and I couldn't help but wonder about the lives of those who had occupied this space just moments earlier.

One of the main risks I had to contend with was the possibility of Iraqi and Kurdish advances not fully clearing some of the villages as they progressed. This meant that there was a credible risk of ISIS fighters popping up from the flanks and the rear. Resistance from ISIS had intensified in recent days, increasing in lethality and their ability to conduct complex attacks and ground assaults, as was witnessed recently in Kirkuk. There was also a substantial threat from VBIEDs, IEDs, mines, and booby-traps.

The following day, Islamic State militants set fire to sulphur stocks at a factory in Mishroq, south of Mosul, creating a plume of sulphur dioxide noxious smoke that drifted over the US airbase in Qayyarah. I purchased extra respiratory protection masks and protective clothing to be carried in each vehicle. We decided to push further west and coordinate with Peshmerga forces across the Al-Khazir. Earlier that morning, on the outskirts of Karemlesh, a VBIED had been detonated, killing eight Peshmerga fighters and wounding up to 20 more. We witnessed the aftermath of the attack, which left vehicles twisted and mangled upon blood-stained ground.

We have been given permission to push further west, past Bartella, to where the Peshmerga are heavily entrenched with a series of bunkers, vehicles, and weaponry, including assault rifles, heavy machine guns, and field guns. Intense fighting has been ongoing all night between the Golden Brigade and Islamic State fighters, including small arms fire, mortars, and IEDs. The Golden Brigade have captured four members of ISIS.

I notice several ambulances returning from the area, carrying wounded Iraqi and Kurdish soldiers. One of the commanders informs us that ISIS fighters have been shaving their beards in an attempt to go unnoticed and that four journalists have recently been injured during the fighting. Dozens of outgoing artillery rounds are being fired over our heads towards Mosul. Heavily entrenched with the Peshmerga Forces in the vast expanse of the arid desert, I spot a vehicle hurtling toward us like a mirage brought to life by the shimmering waves of heat rising from the sun-baked earth. It could almost be an extension of the arid landscape itself. It emerges from the distant horizon, charging through the sands, leaving a trail of dust in its wake. The wheels kick up miniature sandstorms that dance in the truck's turbulent slipstream. Its metallic skin glistens in the intense desert sunlight. There is a thunderous uproar of commotion and panic. "IED! IED! IED! Qunbula!" I then hear the distinctive thunderous burst and guttural roar of an RPG as one of the Peshmerga fighters fires towards the vehicle. The rocket streaks through the air with a high-pitched hiss, and dozens more pepper the vehicle with a volley of automatic fire.

A deafening roar tears through the stillness, then a colossal explosion, a tempest of raw power that sends a shockwave expanding in all directions. It creates ripples in the air and causes the desert sand to levitate momentarily. The vehicle's explosion is felt as a palpable force, a merciless push against the chest. I hunch forward and instinctively wrap both of my arms around my head, as do the rest of the team. It's a primal response to the onslaught. A mushroom cloud begins to ascend, a towering plume of smoke and debris, a monument to the unleashed energy. As the aftermath settles and the landscape bears the scars of a gaping void where silence once reigned, there are deafening cries of "Allahu Akbar! Allah Akbar, Allahu Akbar!" With triumphant exuberance, the unwavering Peshmerga fighters jubilantly dance around after successfully striking their mark, firing celebratory bursts into the sky with their AK-47 rifles.

A journalist from another news team has received a piece of shrapnel to his left arm from the VBIED, and a piece of warped hot shrapnel has embedded into the camera equipment that I'm lying next to. I take a minute to gather my thoughts and then check that the crew is unhurt.

On our way back to the hotel, we pass a truck full of female PKK fighters (a female guerrilla unit of the Kurdistan Workers' Party), travelling west to the front line. Upon our return to the hotel, there are ongoing reports of heavy fighting in Hamdaniya, including up to four VBIEDs, but we call it a day.

The following morning, we successfully made contact with a

Beyond the Drop Zone

representative from the UN Refugee Agency (UNHCR) at Dibaga IDP Camp. The scene that greeted us was one of profound despair etched on the faces of the inhabitants. The sprawling settlement, accommodating up to a staggering one million people, sprawled out before us. A tapestry of makeshift tents stretched to the horizon. Entire families were huddled together in cramped, minuscule quarters, painting a disheartening picture of the hardships they were enduring. It seemed the very essence of hope had been eclipsed by a shadow of anguish, leaving behind a portrait of profound despair. The eyes of the children resembled dimly lit orbs, starved of their radiance, drowning in the depths of sorrow. Though silent, this look spoke volumes of the human spirit's resilience and the yearning for a glimmer of light to pierce through the darkness. Our team interviewed some of the displaced people there, predominantly from Mosul and the surrounding areas.

Before the end of the deployment, we visited a few hospitals in Erbil and spoke with some of the wounded soldiers. As I walked into the theatre, I saw a young boy, maybe nine years old, with severe blast injuries to his chest. He was gasping for breath and looked like he didn't have long left in this world.

The triumphant reclaiming of Mosul from the clutches of the so-called Islamic State came at a harrowing cost, as over 10,000 innocent civilians were killed in the fierce struggle to liberate the city from the caliphate's grip. The city's once-proud edifices now lay in ruins, bearing witness to the profound devastation that had befallen this ancient city.

Beyond the Drop Zone

13: THE HIDDEN EYE

The bustling morning market is already alive with the pulse of vibrant colours and exotic scents. Lively chatter permeates the air, mingling with the enticing aroma of food. Stalls brim with fresh produce like pomegranates and figs, and the scent of sizzling kebabs wafts through the air, tempting passers-by.

In the near distance, piles of colourful fabrics and carpets demand attention. Vendors call out their prices, engaging in spirited bargaining with customers weaving through the crowd. It's a very Eastern symphony, but every so often, a waft of wood smoke curls up from distant villa chimneys. Its smell travels on the breeze, making me think of Britain and a home I've never quite known but that still feels familiar.

Within this picturesque scene, unbeknownst to its inhabitants, a clandestine game of cat and mouse is unfolding on the outskirts. Our target, a woman wearing a tailored black suit and highly polished shoes, exits a café promptly at 8:45 am, adhering to her routine. Confidence exudes from her posture and demeanour, showcasing a poised and assertive presence. I receive confirmation of her movement: "Stand by. Stand by, Echo One Foxtrot." From a distance, I watch as she lights a cigarette and heads toward her parked car.

Covert surveillance involves monitoring activities, gathering information, and observing movements, communications, and interactions. It requires techniques such as physical observation on foot or in a vehicle, electronic monitoring, and video or audio recording. I've been involved in surveillance tasks with teams ranging from two to eight operatives. While I don't recommend solo surveillance, I have done it. Each approach has its own benefits. On this assignment, we were a two-person team with a handler back in the UK. Our task: gather information for a UK client regarding a target suspected of corporate espionage.

Tailing the target on foot poses a high exposure risk. I'm keenly aware of the need to maintain distance, staying out of her '10 to 2' arc of vision and blending in with the morning commuters. My heart races as I navigate the bustling streets, tracking her every move. As we near the hotel complex, Gaz, one of our foot operatives, takes over. "Echo One, now complete. Charlie One, are you okay to take over?" Adrenaline surges through me like a tidal wave, yet I muster every ounce of willpower to remain composed.

The bustling hotel lobby provides excellent cover, affording ample opportunities for me to position myself strategically. Any unusual behaviour or repeated sightings are the main risks of being compromised during surveillance, especially with a small team. I take my time, using a shop window's reflection to assess the environment. With each step, I subtly adjust my posture to appear like any ordinary guest. I also ensure I'm imperceptible to other hotel guests, conscious of the numerous CCTV cameras at the hotel's entrance and reception area where guests are checking in. The hotel windows, acting as my reflective allies, enhance my cover. Inside, I'm focused, merging with the crowd as an inconspicuous observer.

My target, seemingly oblivious to our watchful eyes, meets with a potential lead. The grand hotel's opulent interior, adorned with marble columns and soft lighting, sets the scene. I position myself discreetly, maintaining surveillance through the mirrored reception desk. Nestled within my shoulder bag, a covert camera begins recording as the conversation unfolds over coffee. Just as the target reaches into her bag, a family of tourists obscures my view. "Temporarily unsighted," I inform Gaz. Deciding to reposition, I tactfully make my way to a nearby car rental stand. Regaining visual contact, I begin to feel exposed or 'hot'. I watch the target hand over a small memory stick, and a sense of urgency washes over me. With each passing moment, the risk of exposure looms larger, like a shadow creeping across the pavement. It is a sense of unease that settles in your mind and comes with experience. As the target and her contact gesture to a waiter to settle their bill, I make the decision that it's time to stand down. I send a quick message to Gaz: *"Stand by. Stand down."*

With practiced precision, I disappear into the crowd, melting into the throngs of people milling about the busy hotel lobby. Navigating a maze of narrow alleyways and side streets, I keep a cautious eye out for any signs of compromise. The weight of the covert camera in my bag serves as a reminder of the evidence we've collected—evidence that could potentially unravel a web of deception. Finally reaching the rendezvous point, I meet with Gaz for a quick debrief over a cold beer.

As we make our way back to our hotel on the other end of town, I replay the events of the day in my mind. I question whether we could have done anything differently. The sun sets on another day, casting long shadows across the city streets. I know that our work is far from over. But for now, we'll take solace in the knowledge that today was a success.

Over the years, participating in surveillance operations, both domestically and abroad, has been a multifaceted journey filled with challenges and rewards. The work demands more than just physical stamina; it requires a delicate balance of patience, quick thinking, and unwavering integrity in the face of ever-changing circumstances. Much like in the Paras, moments of high adrenaline and covert manoeuvring are interspersed with stretches of prolonged tedium, whether spent in an observation post or confined to a cramped surveillance van. However, it is within these seemingly mundane intervals that the true essence of the profession becomes apparent. During these times of quiet vigilance, critical insights are often gained, shaping investigations and contributing to the success of the operation. Despite the inevitable hurdles and occasional monotony, the experiences that I gained from such tasks remain uniquely fulfilling. Real-life espionage requires a level of dedication and resolve that no blockbuster movie or spy novel could ever truly convey.

In a dimly lit room tucked away in the heart of a bustling Southeast Asian city, the humidity hangs thick in the air. A palpable presence clings to my skin like a damp but invisible veil. Breathing feels like inhaling the warmth of a tropical evening.

The walls are painted shades of ochre and deep red, their colours muted by the soft glow of the bare bulb hanging delicately from the ceiling. Interwoven with the humidity is the faint, ethereal scent of incense, a fragrance that lingers delicately on the edge of perception, carrying whispers of sandalwood and jasmine. Worn bamboo blinds filter the streetlights through their slats, casting shadows that stretch across the room, accentuating the cracks on the tiled floor.

A low wooden table stands at the room's centre, its surface scattered with the remnants of a hastily eaten meal—crumbled rice grains and a half-empty bottle of now-warm water. In one corner, a rickety ceiling fan hums lethargically, barely stirring the heavy air. Hunched on a plastic stool, I fix my gaze on the glowing light of my phone, my eyes glazed.

After months undercover, my face, roughened by days of stubble, shows the heavy strain of a double life. The room, with its delicate yet worn charm, is both sanctuary and cage—a space where the line between my true self and the persona I project to the world blurs and fades.

I reach into a drawer beside the bed and pull out a small notebook, flipping through pages of scribbled notes and dates recounting various details of the job. I wonder if this way of life is for me anymore. I think of my wife, whom I've left behind, her name feeling like that of a long-lost friend. Even my true identity is becoming an increasingly distant memory.

The weight of the decision presses down on me like the stifling air of the tropical night. I inhale deeply and close the notebook, tucking it away like a forbidden secret. My phone screen continues to flash, briefly illuminating the room with each notification. In those fleeting moments of light, I feel the weight of every falsehood, every concealed truth, bearing down on me. It's then that I come to the realisation that it's time to find a way out of this.

Undercover work involves forming appropriate relationships with individuals involved in a particular activity and maintaining cover whilst gaining intelligence and delivering on the objectives of a broader investigation. It can take place in a diverse range of environments, each with its own unique set of challenges and requirements. From organised crime and corporate settings to terrorist organisations, operatives might attend public gatherings such as rallies, protests, or conventions, as well as social settings like clubs, bars, or social circles.

Developing a robust cover story and gaining a thorough understanding of the environment in which you will be operating is a crucial aspect of the role. It involves subtly influencing perceptions and decisions from behind the scenes, using charm, empathy, and cunning to achieve objectives while maintaining discretion. Key to this is adaptability and a deep grasp of human psychology to shape outcomes and guide actions. This often requires recognising and exploiting others' vulnerabilities, desires, and motivations and skilfully weaving narratives and half-truths to achieve desired result— all of which has its cost.

Maintaining discretion is crucial for protecting individual identities and preserving the integrity of the operations I've been involved in. It's essential that those involved remain safeguarded, which means I must avoid putting myself or anyone I've previously worked with at risk of exposure or compromise.

Many of the skills I developed in the Parachute Regiment, such as performing under pressure and adapting quickly to a rapidly changing environment, have stayed with me. There is an old saying in the PARAs: "No plan survives first contact with the enemy." This highlights the necessity of thinking on your feet, de-escalating challenging situations, and turning the tide to your advantage. These fundamental behaviours became integral to my approach and continue to guide me to this day.

I've been fortunate enough to work undercover in various settings across the world. It's worth mentioning that I likely only scratched the surface of the operations our dedicated police officers, special forces, and other agencies carry out every day. The work can often be extremely dangerous and often thankless, demanding total commitment. The psychological toll can be immense, and I've been privileged to work alongside some of these remarkable individuals, an experience I hold in high regard.

I envisage the future of undercover operations evolving significantly alongside advancements in technology. With developments in surveillance and data analytics, more efficient and accurate monitoring will be enabled through AI-powered facial recognition, drones, and sophisticated data analytics. As criminal activities increasingly move online, cyber operations will become crucial, requiring advanced skills in hacking and cyber-infiltration to track and apprehend cybercriminals. AI- and machine-learning algorithms will assist in analysing vast amounts of data, identifying patterns, predicting criminal behaviour, helping anticipate threats, and making increasingly intelligent and informed decisions on operations.

Advanced secure communication channels will reduce risks to human agents by providing real-time intelligence from dangerous environments, while virtual- and augmented-reality technologies will be used for training, mission planning, and providing comprehensive situational awareness. Despite some of these benefits, challenges such as maintaining operational security, protecting against cyber threats, and ensuring ethical use of surveillance technologies will be critical.

Beyond the Drop Zone

As I sit in that humid, modest room with the rickety fan, surrounded by the muffled sounds of the city—the distant murmur of traffic, occasional laughter from nearby street vendors, and the soft, rhythmic chirping of crickets creating a hypnotic, almost meditative ambiance—I realise it is time to focus on what truly matters to me. I reflect on the childhood I missed out on, shaped by my mother's abandonment and my father's absence due to his work abroad. When I think of my son, I see history starting to repeat itself, and I'm determined to prevent that for his sake. The most important lesson I've learned, one my wife has lovingly taught me, is that family and security should always come first. These, above all else, are the sources of my greatest fulfilment.

14: FIGHTING THE ABYSS

"It's not good news, I'm afraid, Andrew." The white walls of the examination room mirror the harsh fluorescent lights above. The air carries the distinct scent of antiseptic, mingled with the subtle hum of medical equipment. Yet that one sentence cuts straight through the sterile atmosphere. *"You have a rare kidney disease,"* the consultant continues, his tone sombre but empathetic, a balance I assume he's perfected over many years of giving unwanted diagnoses.

I look at him in disbelief. It sounds serious, but I have no idea what it means. *"It's a chronic autoimmune kidney disorder,"* he elaborates. *"The immune system mistakenly targets and damages the kidneys, which are responsible for filtering waste and excess fluids from the blood. In the early stages, it causes blood and protein in your urine, leading to inflammation and scarring of the kidney tissue over time before end-stage renal failure."*

"But I don't feel unwell," I think. Other than noticing some blood in my urine just two weeks after returning from Afghanistan, I feel okay and physically fit. He goes on to explain that the exact cause isn't fully understood but that it's believed to involve a combination of genetic predisposition and environmental factors. Management will involve slowing disease progression and reducing symptoms. There is no cure.

Memories soon flood my mind of those months in Sangin—the gallons of sterilised river water we drank and appalling living conditions we endured. Could those hardships have played a part in this?

Treatment would involve ingesting an abundance of medication every day. Drugs would be prescribed to control my blood pressure and reduce inflammation, and there would be regular monitoring of my kidney function and urine protein levels to assess the disease's progress. My blood pressure was already at Stage 2 hypertension, putting me at greater risk of a life-threatening heart attack or stroke. I didn't understand; I was 22 years old, fit as a butcher's dog, and yet my blood pressure was dangerously high due to the slow build-up of toxins in my blood.

Once again, I found myself contemplating my own mortality. Following two kidney biopsies, I was prescribed dozens of tablets, each with its own side effects, including uncontrollable hand-shaking and heart palpitations. As the disease tightened its grip, my hair, which I was already pulling out in clumps due to stress, now began falling out of its own accord. Each medication and intensive course of steroids affects each patient differently. It took years to get the dosage correct. Every few months, my body would violently mutiny, and I would become so sick that I'd have to spend time in hospital.

In 2015, one such episode left me dangerously unwell. I was in a remote part of Thailand, enjoying some time off. At that time, I was still operating in Iraq as a private security contractor. I would spend a few months in-country on armoured convoys, followed by a few weeks off. I had started Muay Thai training in Thailand and often slept at the gym in extremely basic fighters' dormitories. One evening, after visiting a night market, I thought I'd contracted food poisoning. My breathing became laboured, and my skin turned pale and clammy. Each movement would send waves of pain coursing through my body. It felt like something I'd never experienced before—and I'd experienced a lot by this point. Even the gentlest touch felt like fire against my fevered skin. My hands and feet swelled up like water balloons—I couldn't even get my feet into my sandals.

To make matters worse, I was over 6,000 miles from the UK. I was able to find a back-street clinic after stumbling into a 7-Eleven shop and pleading with a store assistant. Nestled within dark, winding alleys, the weathered medical clinic was adorned with faded paint and cracked signage. Despite being drenched in sweat and drifting in and out of consciousness, I remember the scent of herbal remedies mingling with the musty odour of ageing furniture, and the other patients huddled together on benches worn smooth with time and use. Eventually, I was taken outside and sprawled on a concrete step. My potassium levels were dangerously high, so the staff administered medication to increase potassium excretion through urine and injected insulin to temporarily shift potassium into cells.

Forty-eight gruelling hours later, my symptoms had subsided, though my legs remained severely swollen. I booked a one-way ticket back to the UK to consult with a specialist and assess any heart abnormalities. My brother-in-law, Ray, picked me up from Manchester Airport. I asked him not to tell anyone that I was back and got him to take me directly to the hospital, where I would end up spending the next few weeks.

The chronic symptoms and periods of illness were realities I lived with for years. Yet I was determined not to let this disease dictate my career. I ensured that I had plenty of medication before any deployment and familiarised myself with the locations of hospitals in the countries I was visiting. I saw a renal consultant every three months and managed the treatment I was receiving to the best of my ability.

Months later, I was deployed to the Syrian border, just a few years after the start of the Syrian Revolution, where the United Nations Human Rights Office (OHCHR) reported that nearly 307,000 civilians had been killed. I was working for an organisation, running a HEAT course for independent Syrian journalists. My consultant in the UK had requested a full blood test. He was fantastic, allowing me to continue working in some of the world's most challenging and hostile

Beyond the Drop Zone

environments for nearly 10 years, doing a job that I loved.

Such medical necessities became part of my planning and preparation before deploying anywhere. I would research local clinics in the area, including identifying the nearest hospitals and airports and planning my exit strategy from the country. On this particular trip, I caught a taxi to a medical clinic in nearby Gaziantep, a Turkish town near the Syrian border. This wasn't without its risks, as it was a place where ISIS cells were known to operate. Just weeks prior, a suicide bomber had killed more than 50 guests at a wedding. I encountered some truly bewildered faces when I walked into that clinic and approached the dusty, tired-looking reception desk. Using a combination of broken Turkish and English, I managed to convince the receptionist that I needed a blood test and was able to pay in US dollars. The results were printed off for me in Turkish. I used my phone to take a picture of the blood results and emailed them to my doctor back home, apologising for the language barrier and hoping he would be able to translate.

Despite all of my planning, however, my condition began to deteriorate. With endless appointments at the renal clinic, numerous hospital admissions, and health scares, it became clear that I needed to start thinking about the future.

This wasn't my first brush with a serious illness, either. Just a few years earlier, in 2009, I had been sitting on the cold examination table of a surgical clinic when a doctor, clad in a white coat, had finally broken the silence and diagnosed me with skin cancer—a particularly aggressive form of melanoma. As his words sliced the air like a surgeon's scalpel, my mind reeled, grappling with the stark reality of the diagnosis. The room seemed to sway, and the doctor's words became a distant hum as I struggled to process the enormity of what he was saying. "The prognosis is currently uncertain," he told me, his voice now seeming distant. "We need to explore treatment options, but I won't sugar-coat it; there is going to be a challenging road ahead."

After several surgeries and a skin graft, I was told that I

was cancer-free. Yet the disease would continue to haunt me. Because of my diagnosis, I wouldn't qualify for a kidney transplant for several years.

As a freelance consultant, I was travelling all over the world and making a positive name for myself on the close protection circuit. It was a job that encapsulated everything I was passionate about. It was therefore incredibly challenging for me to have an honest conversation with myself and admit that something had to change. I was witnessing my body slowly deteriorate. Throughout my life, I'd always trained hard and maintained my fitness and strength. When I'd suffered physical injuries, I would adapt my training or use physiotherapy to recover, but this was different. The harsh reality was that I was slowly dying, and I didn't know what the future held. Over the next few harrowing years, I spiralled into a devastating abyss of illness. Hospital corridors became a grimly familiar backdrop. I felt like I was losing my vitality. Where once my skin had been tanned and rugged, it now looked emaciated, taking on a sickly grey-and-yellow pallor. It was a cruel outer embodiment of the disease that was wreaking havoc on my internal organs.

My heart felt as if it was about to burst from the toxins accumulating in my blood. The looming threat of a heart attack or stroke was constant. Death hung over me every bit as much as it had in Iraq and Afghanistan; it seemed to be waiting around every corner, ready to pounce. My lungs betrayed me, leaving me increasingly short of breath. My blood held dangerously low levels of haemoglobin and iron. It felt like I was in a kind of purgatory, caught between something like a waking nightmare and a constant hangover.

Finally, the day came when I fell into complete renal failure. It is said that in the natural world, just before the end, the body purges itself of waste. This was humiliatingly confirmed as I helplessly voided both urine and faeces, a sign that my existence teetered on the brink of oblivion. I was rushed to the local Accident and Emergency Department, where medical marvels unfolded as doctors grappled with my grave condition. The levels of creatinine and toxins in my blood had reached unimaginable heights, and the staff marvelled at how I still clung to life against all odds.

I was in intensive care for 10 torturous days, being subjected to a series of procedures aimed at saving me from impending death. With each passing day, I became acutely aware that this marked the end of my old life. If I survived, what time I had left would not—could not—be the same. Looking back, all I can remember of what was happening around me is lots of needles and masked figures carrying out complex procedures. In the darker moments, it was as if I could feel my body giving way beneath the weight of the trauma it was being asked to cope with. Everything, even life, was slipping beyond my fragile grasp.

But I survived and eventually began haemodialysis, a process that involved a doctor carefully guiding a long tube into the primary artery of my chest. A week later, I was finally discharged from the hospital. For the next eight months, however, I would have to return every other day to watch my blood being cleansed through a machine and returned to my body, akin to sitting in a launderette, staring at a spinning washing machine.

As fate would have it, my sister Julie proved to be a match as a kidney donor. It was a peculiar twist of destiny, reminiscent of the earlier sacrifices she had made for me. As children, our circumstances were far from perfect. Without present parents and with little money, there was a void and a feeling of abandonment. But Julie stepped up and took on the parental role with a bravery that belied her tender age. She sacrificed her personal dreams, her aspirations, her whole life to raise me as her own. Her sacrifices allowed me to grow, explore, learn, and live. Now, all these years later, she was making another sacrifice for me. It wasn't just emotional or financial this time either; it was physical. She was giving one of her kidneys, part of her body, to save me. It was an act of selflessness that filled me with awe and indescribable gratitude.

The day of the transplant dawned. 6th June 2017, my own D-Day. I remember the now-familiar smell of the hospital, the beeping of monitors, and the soft whispers of nurses preparing for various procedures. I remember Julie's hand in mine, her warm, confident grip a stark contrast to the cold, clinical environment around us. She met my gaze, her eyes filled with a strange mix of worry, hope, and fierce determination. "We'll pull through," she said, her voice a steadfast beacon in the storm. I nodded, unable to formulate words around the lump in my throat.

I'd made my stance clear to the staff: I refused to be wheeled into surgery like a piece of luggage. I was going to stride into that cold, sterile operating theatre on my own terms, powered by my own two feet. If I didn't wake up, if that operating table became my final resting place, I wanted my loved ones to remember me as I truly was: resilient and determined to the bitter end. I wanted my wife, my brother Mark, and my sister's husband Ray to hold onto the image of me standing tall in the face of the reaper.

The surgery was a success, the perfect testament to Julie's sacrifice. As I recovered, I couldn't help but marvel at how our lives had intertwined and at Julie's selflessness, from raising me when we were children, to now giving a part of herself to save my life. She had given me a second chance at life, a chance to breathe, to experience the world anew. Already strong, our bond was now cemented by something even more profound and tangible. I am eternally grateful.

After spending a week in hospital post-op, I was relieved to be released. Determined to regain my strength, I found myself doing press-ups on the bedroom floor at home just a few weeks later. It was a small victory, but it marked the beginning of my journey towards recovery. As the days turned into weeks, I pushed myself harder, gradually building up my endurance and stamina. Three months after leaving the hospital, I completed a half-marathon. The funds raised were dedicated to a veterans' mental health charity, advocating for the well-being of those who have served our country.

Looking back, I realise that my journey was not just about personal triumph but about the power of perseverance and the impact we can have on the lives of others. My experience taught me the importance of resilience, compassion, and the ability to turn challenges into opportunities for growth. Today, I continue to advocate for mental health awareness and support for veterans, knowing first-hand the transformative power of determination and the importance of giving back.

15: LOVE'S UNEXPECTED ARRIVAL

Never did I imagine that I would meet someone like her. I felt too burdened by the weight of past traumas clinging to me like a persistent shadow, obscuring any glimmer of light.

My second wife, Louise, a woman moulded by the warmth of a good home and the embrace of a loving family, stands in stark contrast to the turbulent landscape of my own upbringing. She entered my life precisely when I needed her most, bringing with her a sense of warmth and support that allowed me to heal and grow in ways I never thought possible. She comes from a place where dinner tables are laden not just with food but also with laughter and shared stories. Her roots are deeply grounded in the embrace of unconditional love and family.

We first met on a blind date after weeks of messaging back and forth. As the sun began to set on a cold autumn evening in 2014, my train arrived in Manchester. Nervously, I prepared to meet Louise for the first time. To my surprise, she had arrived earlier than me and anxiously waited at the bottom of the long railway station escalators. The mechanical hum of the escalators reverberated through the expansive space, reflecting the pounding rhythm of my heart. The hurried footsteps, voices, and clattering of luggage from the bustling commuters that surrounded us only heightened my apprehension.

Thoughts raced through my mind, questioning whether she would even like me.

Then I caught sight of her, standing there with a nervous smile. We briefly greeted each other and made our way to a cosy whiskey bar just across the road. The warm glow of the dimly lit room embraced us as we exchanged hesitant smiles. Then Louise's vibrant personality immediately filled the space as she spoke with a voice that danced like a melody. "So, how was your journey?" she asked, her eyes sparkling with curiosity.

As we savoured our whiskey cocktails, the smooth liquid leaving behind a trail of warmth, we spent the next few hours getting to know each other even more. Emboldened by the whiskey's embrace, we decided to continue our evening at a nearby German bar. The atmosphere was filled with lively chatter and the clinking of glasses as we entered.

I knew from that moment that Louise was different and that I liked her a lot. Her laughter was infectious, and we raised our large beers in stein glasses, the frothy liquid spilling over the sides, adding to the joyful chaos. We couldn't resist the urge to dance on the tables, our feet stomping to the rhythm of the German *volksmusik*. In that magical moment, nothing else mattered. The world melted away, and it was just Louise and me, completely lost in the euphoria of the night.

Lou is a woman whose presence radiates beauty and kindness. With long chestnut-brown hair cascading over her shoulders, she possesses an undeniable natural beauty. Her infectious laugh brightens any room, and she has inviting lips and the distinct charm of a northern accent, which carries a comforting familiarity.

When we first started dating, I was still working as a team leader on armed protection convoys in Iraq, a job that demanded long stretches away from home. Saying goodbye during those early days, with the uncertainty of a prolonged absence, was a challenge that spurred introspection. Daily Skype calls and text messages bridged the miles, yet the toll on relationships and the life I aspired to build made me question the compatibility of my future with the demands of this line of work. During the precious time I had off, we transformed mundane moments into unforgettable adventures. We travelled to exotic destinations, and we explored charming cities across the UK.

A particularly memorable second date was at an indoor ski slope near Manchester, where we were both living. Aware of Lou's passion for skiing, my own expertise was limited to a distant military exercise in Canada. However, armed with determination and a desire to impress, I chose not to disclose my lack of proficiency on the piste. As we geared up for the slope, I tried to mirror Lou's confidence. "Have you both skied here before?" a member of staff inquired. Without missing a beat, I confidently replied, "Oh yeah, I've been here a few times," successfully masking my novice status. The impending challenge of a 180-metre-long main slope, towering at 40 metres, loomed ahead. Undeterred, I convinced myself that mastering the art of skiing couldn't be that difficult—I was an ex-Para after all. Little did I know that this impromptu adventure would become a hilarious test of my adaptability and courage.

Standing at the top of the slope, there was no backing down. I took off, my speed increasing with every second, passing other skiers as a blur. I desperately attempted to slow my descent, but nothing seemed to work. Accepting my impending fate, I fell back on the parachute landing training I'd learned all those years ago: "Stay tight and accept the landing," I reminded myself. Forcefully bringing both skis together, I turned to one side, leaned back into the slope, and braced as tight as I could. I began tumbling in a spectacular fashion, only coming to a stop when I hit the cushion crash barrier at speed. I lay there for a moment, dazed. Lou elegantly glided over to me, her expression equally shocked and amused as she glanced down at me and said, "I thought you said you'd skied before?" Shortly after, a member of staff asked me to leave the slope as I was deemed unsafe. I couldn't really argue with that.

We shared common interests in country music, old rock and roll, blues, food, and travel. Yet I found myself in a place I felt was undeserving of such a connection. There were and are challenges when gremlins of the past desire to resurface. My darkest experiences occurred in a world that is alien to Louise, but she continually surprises me with her patience, support, and understanding. It's a world she never chose to be a part of, yet she has embraced it with grace and resilience. She held an unwavering belief in me when I faltered, and I often wonder whether I would have made it at all without her support and guidance. It is a story of togetherness that transcends time and circumstance.

Too many soldiers today are struggling. They're backed into a corner with little or no support network and are unsure where to turn. I am glad that we're slowly seeing a positive change in the narrative surrounding mental health, and male mental health in particular. There certainly is plenty of support out there, but sometimes, you will need that nudge. We all have a crucial role to play in that—a responsibility to reach out and check in with one another, offering a listening ear and a helping hand to those who may be struggling in silence. My brother once said to me that people will often say that they didn't call simply because they didn't know what to say or how to start the conversation. Well, if that is the case, just say exactly that. Just pick up the phone and listen. Say that you don't know what to say. It goes a long way.

Never underestimate the power of a simple phone call, the impact of a few words spoken from the heart. Let yourself be the nudge that someone needs, the reminder that they are not alone in their journey. In the end, it is our connections with one another that sustain us and give meaning to our lives in the face of challenges. And in that shared journey, we find strength, resilience, and the power to overcome even the darkest of days.

16: THE FIRE SERVICE

To me, being a firefighter is more than just a job; it offers a sense of belonging and purpose. It's a commitment to something greater than oneself. A deep connection to a close-knit group or community can have a profound effect on human well-being. Finding direction and a sense of belonging became a lifeline, especially after leaving the military—a transition many soldiers struggle with. The close-knit groups I became a part of offered essential emotional support, often in ways we didn't even recognise at the time. Belonging to these groups helped reduce the loneliness that can be so overwhelming, fostering the strong sense of identity and community that I'd been searching for. There's something incredibly valuable in being able to vent to a colleague or share a joke; these simple acts build positive, supportive networks that provide effective coping mechanisms. Without them, the isolation can be devastating.

  The job can sometimes mean stepping into the heart of chaos when everything around you is falling apart. It can mean running into a burning building with smoke billowing out of the windows at three o'clock in the morning to drag a family overcome by smoke to safety. It can mean cutting a driver out of the mangled mess of sharp edges and contorted steel of a car accident in the pouring rain, the vehicle's structure bent beyond recognition on the side of a motorway. But you know you can make a difference—your actions can turn the tide in the darkest of moments. It's about rushing towards danger when every instinct is screaming at you to do what everyone else is doing and run the other way. Yet, in those moments, I find a strange clarity. I become hyper-aware of each breath, each movement, as time seems to stretch and compress in surreal ways. The acrid taste of smoke lingers in the air, mingling with the almost suffocating sensation of the facemask pressed tightly against my face. The heat is relentless, even through the thick layers of robust protective clothing. The weight of responsibility presses down on my shoulders, demanding not just safety, but also the precision needed to prevent the incident from escalating.

Teamwork, trust, and unwavering dedication to the firefighters who sit on that pump with you and those who turn out on the incident ground with you are non-negotiable characteristics of the job. It's knowing that your safety depends on their actions just as much as theirs depends on yours. There is a camaraderie, much like that of soldiers, forged through intense training, shared experiences, and continual learning. There is an understanding and anticipation that the next call could be the most challenging yet. It's also about the emotional toll—witnessing the devastating aftermath of road traffic collisions, house fires, drownings, and the pain of those who can't be saved or who lose everything in one night. Each of these incidents leaves a small mark on you.

In late 2018, Lou was already an administrator in the fire service and suggested that a career with them might be a good fit for me. She knew that working in cohesive teams, the camaraderie, and the occasional adrenaline rush of high-pressure, life-threatening situations would appeal to me. And she was right. The range and diversity of incidents we tackle are extensive. With the rising number of vehicles on the roads, we respond to as many road traffic collisions as we do house fires. Our responsibilities span water incidents, hazardous materials, rope rescues, and medical emergencies, including, unfortunately, the growing number of suicides.

The selection course was 16 weeks long, and I found myself to be one of the older recruits. Many aspects of the course resembled those of the military, which for me was now many years ago. Physiology Day is something that all firefighters will remember. The aim of the scenario is simple: to push recruits to their physiological and mental limits. This is achieved through exposure, in a carefully controlled manner, to extreme heat and exhaustion. In full fire gear, including breathing apparatus (BA) weighing around 12 kg under air, you are given two rolled-up 25-metre lengths of 70-mm hose (weighing a further 15 kg each), to carry by your side for the duration of the exercise. You're then instructed to enter a building that has been set alight. Bins are utilised to increase the temperature and replicate a commercial building fire. It's hot inside, like wearing all of your warm clothing and exercising inside a scorching hot sauna with a facemask mask on. It's suffocating and uncontrollable.

As a group, with your lengths of fire hose, you begin walking in continuous loops of a commercial building, up and down metal stairs and across landings, until you finally reach the door you came in through. You then repeat the process until you can't go on. Recruits 'drop off' and quit throughout. The idea of the scenario is not to last to the end, but to know your limits. If you push yourself to the point of hyperthermia and collapse, you are not only putting yourself at risk but also endangering the firefighters who have to find and rescue you.

It turned out that Louise was spot-on, as usual. I found immense satisfaction in every aspect of the job and consider myself extremely fortunate to have discovered a profession that I am genuinely passionate about. In the end, being a firefighter is a testament to the human spirit's capacity for sacrifice and compassion. It's a reminder that even in the face of the fiercest flames, the greatest strength comes from within you and the people around you.

The station I'm based at covers what are considered some

of the grimmest corners of Manchester. North Manchester and Salford have become practically synonymous with gangs and gun crime in recent years, ranking among the UK's worst-affected areas. Substandard social housing has become a breeding ground for antisocial behaviour, and predictably, this has translated into a surge of fire-related incidents and medical emergencies, from stolen cars meeting fiery crashes to arson and drug-related violence and dependency.

It's a scorching July day. I have just two years in the job under my belt, hardly a substantial stretch by any measure. We are sitting eating lunch together when suddenly, the alarm tones pierce through loudspeakers, signalling that we are 'turning out'—fire service lingo for responding to an incident. We dash to the engine house, snatching up the turn-out sheet along the way. This piece of paper holds key details about the incident—type, location, and any casualties that might be involved.

The sheet reads, "Building fire, domestic, persons reported." The latter term indicates that someone is believed to be trapped inside a building and requires rescuing. It is a life-risk emergency. As we gear up and crack the cylinders of our BA sets, the radio comes to life again, with Fire Control adding urgency to the situation. They report "repeat calls" and detail the severity of the blaze. The building is fully alight, and we know that we'll be going in. At that moment, my mind is racing. It's a constant stream of mental chatter, each idea jostling for attention, creating a sense of urgency. What equipment will we need from the fire appliance? How many potential casualties are there? Is there any more information about the property? Are there any witnesses?

As we navigate our way through the traffic, sirens blaring, I look across the rear cab to Dan, my BA partner. He's dependable and robust. His extensive knowledge is matched only by his unwavering reliability in high-pressure situations. "I'll grab the door-ram pal," I say. "You get the reel off." With a faint nod, he replies, "Roger that. Chuck me your tally, and I'll stick it in the board." The board records crucial data about BA wearer when inside a house fire, such as your cylinder contents and how many minutes until your low-pressure whistle actuates.

A chaotic scene awaits us when we turn in to the road: flames and smoke are pulsating from the front bedroom window. Family members and neighbours are on the pavement and in the road, their screams and cries filling the air. Quickly assessing the situation, I take in the blazing building. It's a two-storey end-terrace with PV panels on the roof, a bay window at the front, two windows above—likely the fire compartment—and a bathroom. Dan and I sprint towards the front door, armed with the branch and gaining-entry gear, while the driver assists in unravelling the reel from the drum at the side of the appliance. The door, solid and locked, challenges our urgency. Muscles tensed, I position myself wide and, with calculated force, swing the door ram. The impact splinters the wood, but the door remains stubbornly closed. Undeterred, I take a second swing, and then a third. The damaged door still won't give.

Gasping for air within my facemask, I pass the door ram to Dan, who takes up the assault with a determined series of bangs. The door, reinforced from the inside with various bolts and locks, reveals the harsh reality of tactics often employed by gang members or drug sellers. To complicate matters further, we realise they've potentially rigged improvised booby traps as deterrents for anyone attempting to force their way in. "Fucking great," I mutter under my breath, acutely aware that this job is going to prove even more challenging and dangerous than we thought.

Switching to hydraulic spreaders, we finally gain access. Thick, acrid smoke billows down the wooden-framed staircase, suffocating the air with its oppressive presence. The smoke seems to possess a tangible weight, pressing down on everything in its path, obscuring vision, and choking the breath out of anyone caught in its grasp. Its dense, swirling tendrils dance in the flickering light of the flames, casting eerie shadows on the walls as they descend, signalling the relentless advance of a raging inferno. Using the right-hand wall as a landmark, we navigate up the staircase, meticulously sweeping every inch of space for a body. Upon reaching the top, we confront a cluster of cables and wiring waiting to ensnare us.

Time is against us, and I can feel the fire's heat searing against my outer jacket. Dan unleashes two prolonged pulses of water into the scorching fire gases, providing a momentary respite from the intense temperature. On my hands and knees, I methodically search the two rooms to my right for any signs of life. One is a bedroom, the other a small bathroom. Both are clear. Advancing along the landing, we glimpse the fire room at the corridor's end. It's a cannabis grow operation: three large rooms filled with cannabis plants, tampered electrics, and heating

elements above. Dan attacks the fire while I continue scouring the floor space for bodies.
   Eventually, we manage to knock back and then extinguish the fire. Later, we learn that as we'd entered the building, the occupier had leapt from a rear room window, breaking his leg upon landing. In doing so, he'd left behind his teenage son, who miraculously managed to find a way out on the ground floor through a window and escape. Although suffering from smoke inhalation, he is relatively unscathed. His dad is arrested by police and taken to hospital.

The fire service is a career that I have found to be unpredictable and profoundly rewarding. Each day brings a new challenge, a fresh incident that tests both your skills and your decision-making. The variety of incidents encountered are unparalleled and each one brings their own challenges. This unpredictability, while daunting, is what makes the profession uniquely intriguing and endlessly fulfilling. You never know if that next call will be the biggest of your life. You are more than just an emergency responder; you can be a beacon of hope on what can often be the worst day of someone's life. The ability to alleviate someone's distress, to bring relief in their time of desperation, is an honour few can claim. The skills taught and the knowledge gained all culminate in those moments when you can truly make a difference.
   And on this journey, you are never alone. There are familiarities in the bonds forged with your crew similar to those of the military. In the face of adversity, these bonds of brotherhood and sisterhood are strengthened, making your team not just a group of colleagues, but a closely-knit family, forming relationships that transcend the confines of the job. Being a firefighter is an opportunity where you can make a tangible difference. It's a career that, despite its challenges, makes every risk worthwhile, and it's one that I feel immensely privileged to be a part of.

17: QUEST FOR PURPOSE

As I conclude this memoir, I find myself deeply immersed in reflections on the winding journey that has led me to this moment—a journey marked by self-discovery, resilience, and gratitude. The pursuit of a meaningful life has been a source of inspiration through the peaks and valleys of my experiences. Along that path, I've stumbled upon a profound truth: that meaning is not some grand epiphany but a myriad of small moments that populate our daily lives—moments of quiet conversation, shared laughter, and simple acts of kindness, each contributing to the richness of a purpose-driven existence.

I refuse to see myself as a victim. Instead, I proudly wear the badge of a survivor. Confronting the sacrifices made by countless young men and women and grappling with the fragility of life itself forced me to reassess everything I held dear. It compelled me to redefine concepts like courage, service to one's country, and the notion of belonging to something greater than yourself. Along the way, I discovered the profound power of friendship, brotherhood, and sisterhood. In the midst of chaos, conflict, and suffering, I have borne witness to the extraordinary feats of ordinary individuals—siblings supporting one another, spouses navigating uncertainty together, interpreters and fixers risking their lives daily, and healthcare workers in conflict zones striving to save lives amidst dire conditions. Survival has come at a significant cost. I've weathered storms that threatened to engulf me, emerging stronger. Life's unpredictable twists and turns taught me the art of adaptation and revealed the human spirit's incredible inherent strength. Each scar etched upon my being tells a story of survival and the indomitable will to overcome adversity.

I harbour profound gratitude for those who have walked beside me, for having the honour to serve alongside some extraordinary people, and for the moments of pure joy that have pierced through the darkness. It's a recognition of life's interconnectedness—a realisation that every individual and experience, no matter how fleeting, played a role in shaping the person I have become.

Carrying within me an abiding sense of gratitude for the privilege of leading a complex yet undeniably meaningful life, I view this journey not as a destination but as an ongoing adventure that is fuelled by purpose, defined by resilience, and anchored in gratitude. As I step boldly into the unwritten chapters that lie ahead, I embrace whatever the future may hold, armed with purpose and a profound appreciation for the journey thus far.

I am a proud veteran, a loving husband, and a doting father, but beneath the surface, I am also a man still wrestling with the ghosts of my past. There's a raw, haunting beauty in my story, but my struggle is not unique. Countless other men and women bear the invisible scars of service. PTSD wears many masks, and it bestows a burden too heavy for anyone to carry alone. The harsh reality is that we are losing too many of our brothers and sisters to suicide, a fact that is as heartbreaking as it is preventable.

Back in 2011, I took a bold step towards addressing this issue by pursuing a psychology degree, driven by a burning desire to help other veterans grappling with their mental health. The journey was cut short due to unforeseen circumstances, but it's a path I hope to revisit in the future.

There is help out there, in the form of organisations and charities dedicated to supporting veterans. My plea to anyone wrestling with mental health issues is this: reach out. You are not alone. The world is full of people ready to stand by your side, to listen, help, and remind you that it's okay not to be okay. The first step is acknowledging that there's a problem. It can be the hardest step because it requires admitting vulnerability, but it's crucial for progress. Reach out to your family, friends, or fellow veterans about your struggles. I repeat: you are not alone, and you don't have to face it alone. Sharing your experiences and feelings with others can provide emotional relief and strengthen your support network.

After a difficult job in the fire service, I often find that the best kind of therapy can be dark humour, as it moderates stress. Changing the narrative about a stressful situation can sometimes reduce the physiological stress response. We sit down with a cup of tea, talk, and change the trajectory of an emotional response with dark humour. Subtly, we are unconsciously 'checking in' with each other. There is enormous value in collectively talking about a shared experience.

There's also lots of professional help out there where experts can diagnose your condition accurately, guide you through your recovery journey, and provide effective treatment options. Prioritising self-care activities can help manage symptoms and improve your overall well being. This includes maintaining a healthy lifestyle, getting regular exercise, practising mindfulness or meditation, ensuring adequate sleep, and exploring your creativity—perhaps even writing! I've found that, by educating myself around mental health and understanding my own triggers, I've helped manage symptoms and reduce any stigma in my own mind.

Healing takes time. There are no quick fixes. Celebrate small victories along the way, and remember that it's okay and normal to have bad days. Every individual's journey through mental health recovery is unique, so what works for one person might not work for another. It's crucial to remain patient, persistent, and optimistic throughout the process. Let's brave this storm together as a community, for in our unity lies strength.

Beyond the Drop Zone

ABOUT THE AUTHOR

Andrew Williams joined The Parachute Regiment at the age of 16. After seven years of distinguished service, he transitioned to working in domestic counter-intelligence in the British capital. He then spent a decade working in close protection, specialising in counter-terrorism, bodyguarding, and undercover operations. Andrew went on to work in high-risk consultancy, providing personal security and crisis management expertise to the media, government agencies, and NGOs all over the world.

Printed in Great Britain
by Amazon

78fb7dc6-84ee-499f-afd6-94f5ff41c178R01